Walk! Mercer Island

The Insider's guide to walking on Mercer Island

By Kris Kelsay

Walk! Mercer Island is the comprehensive guide to walking the extensive and beautiful parks, open space, residential neighborhoods and community trails available on the little island, in the middle of Lake Washington. Author Kris Kelsay, an avid walker, hiker, and outdoor enthusiast guides you along this little known and underutilized trail system, pointing out Mercer Island's unique history, beautiful public art, and fascinating flora & fauna along the way. Residents and visitors alike will gain inside knowledge and access to this gem of an Island in Seattle's backyard.

Walk! | Mercer Island
P.O. Box 1658
info@walkmercerisland.com
www.walkmercerisland.com

Dedicated to my favorite
walking buddies—Connor, Shea and Todd—
who find simple delight outdoors, every day.

Introduction

Years ago, when I first moved to Mercer Island, I picked up a green photocopied trail guide from the local drugstore and started exploring the Island on foot. Those hand drawn maps and simple descriptions led me to places that still marvel me today. I've kept that guide—now dog-eared, marked and tattered— and for close to 20 years, have waited for another more current version to appear. It never did.

Later, when my daughter went to pre-school at Sunnybeam School and I met founder Nukie Fellows, I became interested in the history of the place I call home. I picked up the one definitive history book of Mercer Island from Island Books— Judy Gellatly's Mercer Island History—and have read and re-read the stories of the unique rural background of the Island. Many times I've pondered the dramatic changes our Island has experienced over not so many years. I had heard stories about the Mercer Island community that once was, from many long time residents, and was fascinated with what it had become. My walks started to take on new dimensions—"Oh, that must be the Clarke family of Clarke Beach", "These must be apple trees from the Old's Family Homestead," "I wonder who Fluery is of Fluery Trail?"

Still later, when my son was in 2nd grade studying the local history of Mercer Island, I researched the public art on the Island as an art docent lesson—and was amazed at how much great, public art surrounded us. I created a lesson, complete with a guided "Art Walk" for his class and saw the kid's eyes light up when they came upon the art that they now knew.

Then my husband transitioned careers, now heading the transportation department for the Mercer Island School District. Suddenly, bus ridership statistics, "walk zones", "hazard zones", "walking school buses" and "safe walk to school initiatives" became part of my vernacular. As my kids grew up, I thought about the safety of the routes they would take by bike or by foot to the places they go—to school, to the library, to friends. The cut-thrus and paths I'd taken for so many years often provided the safest and most direct routes for them.

Recently, I've been puzzled when my hard-core walking and running friends didn't know about the trails and cut-thrus in their own backyard. Then I realized they have become much harder to find. There is no guide available and many of the path signs have disappeared or been hidden with strategically placed landscaping or a potted plant; and some have simply become inaccessible, period.

When our family travels to a new city, I almost always pick up a walking guide. I love to read about the place I'm seeing, as I see it. I decided that Mercer Island needed its own walking guide—sort of a local's guide that helps people get around by foot and connect with their community in a new way. Walk! Mercer Island is intended to bring the Island alive for people on foot. I hope that you enjoy it.

See you on the trails!

"Walking is a man's best medicine."

Hippocrate

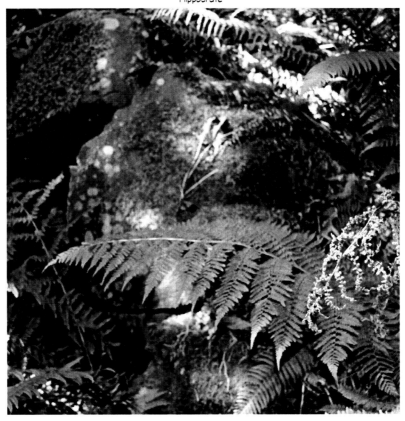

Table of Contents

"Walking is the best possible exercise. Habituate yourself to walk very far."
Thomas Jefferson

Using this Guide

This guide is intended to help you get out on foot, exploring all that Mercer Island has to offer. With 475 acres of parks and open spaces, more than 50 miles of hiking trails and 30 developed and semi-developed parks, there is plenty to see. Behind many of these places, there is a rich history to be discovered, and along the way, there is incredible art, flora and fauna to experience.

Book Sections

There are three main sections in this guide, each with a little different angle to walking on Mercer Island.

Section One: Trail Guide
This section is all about giving you the information you need to use the public trail system on Mercer Island to its full extent—all by yourself. This section graphically shows you the location of all of the official public trails and cut-thrus on the Island, as well as the parks, open space, street ends and other places of interest nearby.

Section Two: Guided Walks
This section contains 12 guided walks that span the Island's geography, and range in difficulty. Think of them as a series of walking tours that guide you along the route giving you information about the history, art, flora and fauna you'll see along the way.

Section Three: From Here to There
On an Island that's only 6.2 square miles total, everything is very close when you're on foot. It's just a matter of knowing how to get there! This section gives you some great routes to get from here to there with turn-by-turn directions and a map to make it easy.

Definitions

This guide explores the parks, open space, street-ends and cut-thrus on the Island—and the interconnected web of trails that connects them all.

Parks	Boy do we have great parks here and they come in all shapes, sizes and styles. They range from Luther Burbank Park—the granddaddy of parks on the North End of the Island, to the very unique Lid Park that tops our freeway, to the forested playground at Deanne's Children's Park, to the myriad of tiny, hidden neighborhood parks. All are worth exploring.
Open Space	Over 300 acres on Mercer Island are designated as Open Space, which is mostly forested. Many have wonderful trails that, in moments, take you away from the stresses of the city. Pioneer Park is the biggest, but each is unique. The city has an Open Space Vegetation Plan to manage these wonderful areas.
Cut-thrus	There are dozens and dozens of little "connector paths" on the Island that make getting from one place to another easier. When I first moved to the Island, they were all marked with little blue "path" signs, but today the signs are less reliable. I call these "cut-thrus" because while they are officially accessible to the public, they generally skirt someone's private property and connect one street to another.
Street-Ends	There are twenty "street ends" on the Island which offer waterfront access to the public—totaling six acres of land and 1,140 feet of water frontage. Some are developed with benches, picnic tables, and parking and others are not. All are great points for viewing, taking off in a kayak, or cooling your feet on a hot day.

What to Wear

In the dry summer months, you will do fine in tennis shoes (even white ones), shorts and a hat anywhere on the Island. The rest of the year, you'll want to be a little more prepared with a pair of light hiking shoes, a hat and a rain coat with a hood. But don't let bad weather scare you off. When it's not summer, the trails do get muddy and the trees drip big drops, but with a good raincoat, some of the best walks can be had in the woods of Mercer Island off-season. The trees bring natural shelter from the wet when it's raining, incredible color during the fall and remarkable quiet during the first snow. My only warning is stay clear of the forests during our famous wind storms—just not a good place to be.

Bringing Along Your Kids

Definitely bring the kids along. There is so much to see and they will help you rediscover the Island in brand new ways through their unique perspective—such a great way to hang out and be active. Many of the main paths in the public parks, and most of the cut-thrus and street ends are accessible with a stroller, but in the Open Space areas, leave the stroller at home. The guided walks found later in this book that are rated as Family Walks are great for little hikers—and I've been sure to point out the location of bathrooms along the way—critical to a successful family walk!

Bringing Along Your Dog

You'll see plenty of dogs on the Mercer Island trails—so feel free to bring yours along. There are two Off Leash Areas (OLAs) on Mercer Island—one great one at Luther Burbank Park, and a second on the south end at Wildwood Park. Dogs must be on a leash at all times in the rest of Luther Burbank Park, the northeast quadrant of Pioneer Park and Deanne's Children's Park. Everywhere else, dogs must be on a leash or under voice or signal control.

Although it seems impossible, some walkers may not like your pooch as much as you do, so make sure they don't approach those that are sharing the parks and paths with you. Also, dogs are not allowed on any public school ground or playground at any time, on sport fields when organized activities are in progress, or in public swimming areas from May 1 to Sept 30th.

Walking Safety

Many of the streets on Mercer Island are quiet and have few cars, but some can present some real challenges. Here are some recommendations for keeping safe:

- When walking on a street with a sidewalk, use it. When walking on a road without a sidewalk (which is very common) walk on the side of the road, against traffic.

- On East, West and North Mercer walk against traffic and keep an the lookout for bikers that travel fast, sometimes with their heads down. A little "heads up" call if they don't appear to see you is prudent.

- When walking along Island Crest Way, be careful of drivers trying turn into traffic from side streets. They often are focused on finding a hole in the traffic and don't notice when you approach. When crossing Island Crest be especially vigilant—the two lanes combined with commuter traffic can make this a bit scary. Be sure to get eye contact with the drivers in both lanes before making the dash.

- When crossing major roads, always use the crosswalk.

- When on the I-90 Trail (a major multiuse path), stay to the right. The fast moving bikes will pass you on your left with a little call.

- I don't recommend walking at night, but if you do, be sure to wear reflective clothing and bring a flashlight.

"These boots are made for walking, and that's just what they'll do."
Lee Hazelwood

Section One
Trail Guide

This section is all about giving you the information you need to use the public trail system on Mercer Island to its full extent—all by yourself. Sometimes it's difficult to see where a trail starts or to know where it will lead; it's hard to tell if it's on public or private land; sometimes it's easier to simply go the way you know. This section is intended to change all of that.

The trails identified in this guide are only those open to the public on public rights of way. They include trails that exist in public parks, on roads, within open space tracts or through conservancy easements of private property. Except in the case of trails within public parks, the public is only entitled to pass through on the trail. Remember to respect the privacy of the homeowners and act like you'd like others to act if they were heading through what feels like your yard. I haven't included the hundreds of 'non-official' trails—I'll leave those for you to find and ask permission to cross, on your own!

The Trail Guide section of the book is divided by geography. There are four sections:

The maps overlap slightly allowing you to orient yourself from map to map. Each geography has a map, a directory of the parks, open space and street ends in the section, and a listing of places of interest and public art you'll find in your travels.

A few things that will help you use the maps:

Trails, Trail Systems and Cut-Thrus are shown on the map with a dotted line
like this: ▪ ▪ ▪ ▪ ▪ ▪

They are also marked with a number which can be found in the accompanying Trails and Cut-Thru Table.

They look like this:

Parks and Other Places of Interest are also listed in a table and are marked in text on the map.

Trail Guide | North End—West

There's a lot going on here on the west side of the North End—big, highly accessible parks and trails, great public art, tons of history, and of course the town center. Things are surprisingly close when you go on foot—with old trails that were traveled way back when the car may not have been an option.

North End—West Trail Map

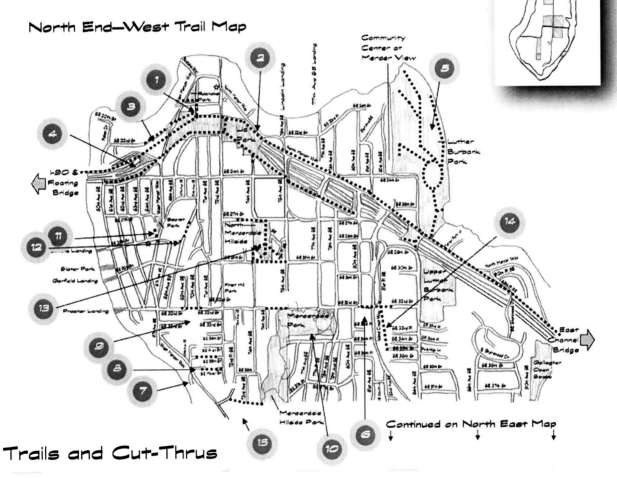

Trails and Cut-Thrus

1	Roanoke Park Trail	8	SE 35th St Cut-Thru (poor condition)
2	I-90 Trail	9	SE 32nd St Cut-Thru
3	SE 22nd Street Cut-Thru	10	Mercerdale Park Trails
4	Lid Park Trails	11	Secret Park Trail
5	Luther Burbank Park Trails	12	68th Ave Cut-Thru
6	Denny Trail	13	North Mercerdale Hillside Trails
7	Maker Street Cut-Thru (poor condition)	14	81st Pl Cut-Thru
		15	72nd Pl Cut-Thru

Trail Guide | North End—East

This section of the island is activity central. With the city buildings, schools, the pool, theater, library and playing fields all within a half mile of each other, and the addition of the Boys and Girls Club PEAK Center in the next few years—it will continue to be a youth hub. So there are a lot of reasons to walk around here.

North End—East Trail Map

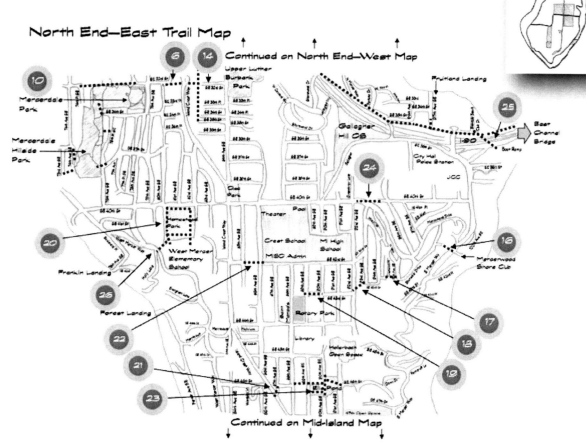

Continued on North End—West Map

Continued on Mid-Island Map

Trails and Cut-Thrus

6	Denny Trail		20	Homestead Trails
10	Mercerdale Trails		21	87th Cut-Thru
14	81st Pl Cut-Thru		22	42nd Cut-Thru
16	Shoreclub Trail		23	Ellis Pond Trails
17	95th & Crestwood Cut-Thru		24	40th St Cut-Thru
18	93rd & 92nd Cut-Thru		25	Boat Ramp Trail
19	43rd Cut-Thru		26	80th Ave SE Cut-Thru

Trail Guide | Mid-Island

Mid-Island is home to some great parks that are easily reached on foot. This section of the island is only a mile wide at its smallest point—unfortunately, you need to cross Island Crest Way on insanely dangerous, four-lane crosswalks to make real use of the east-west access trails. Go early, late or be super careful; and (here's the blatant plea) lobby our City Council to figure out some way to make the area more accessible by foot.

Mid-Island Trail Map

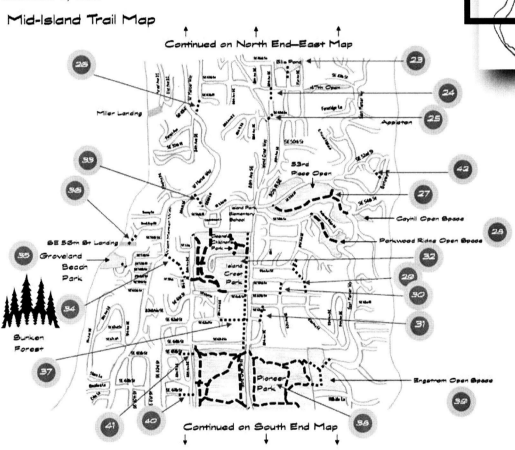

Trails and Cut-Thrus

23	Ellis Pond	33	SE 53rd Cut-Thru
24	89th St Cut-Thru	34	SE 59th Cut-Thru
25	SE 48th St Cut-Thru	35	Groveland Park Trails
26	SE 47th St Cut-Thru	36	SE 56th Landing Trail
27	SE 53rd St OS Trails	37	Stevenson's Trail
28	Parkwood Ridge OS Trails	38	Pioneer Park Trails
29	92rd Cut-Thru	39	Engstrom OS Trails
30	90th Cut-Thru	40	SE 67th Cut-Thru
31	61st St Cut-Thru	41	SE 65th Cut-Thru
32	Island Crest Park Trails	42	Butterworth Cut-Thru

Trail Guide | South End

The south end is home to acres of gorgeous woodland, lovely flat walking, lots of hidden trails, a cozy coffee shop, and some history of its own. Easy walking with the least traffic on the island makes the South End perfect for an outing.

South End Trail Map

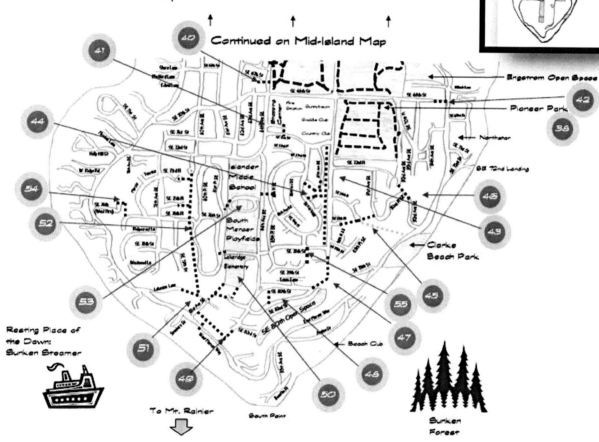

Continued on Mid-Island Map

Trails and Cut-Thrus

38 Pioneer Park Trails	48 SE 80th Cut-Thru
40 67th St Cut-Thru	49 Fluery Trail
41 Shopping Center Cut-Thru	50 Lakeridge Trails
42 SE 68th St Cut-Thru	51 Lakeview Lane Trail
43 Island Crest Way Trail	52 80th Ave SE Trail
44 Wildwood Park Trails	53 IMS Trails
45 SE 77th Cut-Thru	54 West Firs Trail
46 Clarke Beach Trail	55 79th St Cut-Thru
47 Island Crest Cut-Thru	

9

"It's impossible to walk rapidly and be unhappy."
Mother Theresa

Section Two

Guided Walks

This section of the book contains 12 walks that span the Island's geography, and range in difficulty. Think of them as a series of walking tours that should help you make useful connections between the more obvious park trails and places on the Island with some interesting facts thrown in along the way. Generally, they show some of the most desirable ways to get from here to there.

I hope through these hikes to make it easy for families, walkers and runners to explore our Island and make discoveries along the way—new paths that make far places close, new historical facts that bring alive our past, and hints about where to look for the hidden natural beauty of our island. Maybe try one each weekend, bringing this guide along as you travel the trail for the first time. Soon, they will be a part of your Mercer Island vernacular.

You can walk or run all of them year-round with trail shoes; those that can be walked without ruining your nice white tennis shoes, or can accommodate a stroller or bike have been noted. Once you've done them all, you'll have all the knowledge you'll need to get from here to anywhere on the island.

A few things that will help you with this section:

- Each walk has an overview section that lists the rating, length, terrain, highlights and starting point of the walk, along with a map with the walk marked by a series of dots ●●●. It also includes "Turn-by-Turn" directions—for those that want to skip the intellectual stimulation and just get on with the walk or hike.

- The overview section is followed by a "Guided Tour"—for those that like to learn about what they're seeing as they go. To help you follow along, directions for the walk have been written in **bold**, while information about the history, art, flora and fauna are written in normal font.

- The walks have been classified as Family Hikes, Moderate Hikes and Ambitious Hikes. Family Hikes are great for even the littlest hikers and the grandparents. They tend to have fun things to do along the way, are fairly flat and short, and have good restroom access (critical!). Moderate Hikes are a bit longer—often having some elevation change, and Ambitious Hikes are for those looking to spend some time outside getting get some serious exercise.

"Everything is within walking distance if you have the time."
Steven Wright

List of Walks

Family Walk |
East Seattle History Loop

This family hike makes Mercer Island history fun! It's full of unique hidden treasures, great parks, enormous views and places to get wet. Wear tennis shoes, bring the stroller or the dog—even a picnic—and build in some time to hang out at the parks along the way. The hike is all on paved pathways or residential streets.

Rating: Family

Length: 2.75 miles

Terrain: Quiet residential streets and paved paths.

Highlights: Historical sites, great parks, huge waterfront views.

Trailhead: Start at the Boys and Girls Club on SE 28th Street and West Mercer Way

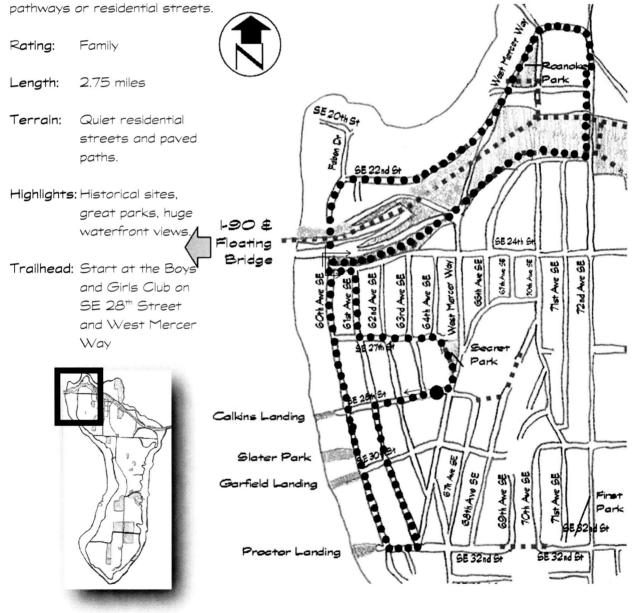

Guided Walk: East Seattle History Loop

0.0 mi   **This walk starts at the Boys and Girls Club on the corner of SE 28ᵗʰ St and 63ʳᵈ Ave SE. From the back lot, take a left on SE 28ᵗʰ, heading toward the water and then take another left on 61ˢᵗ Ave SE.**

The area we are walking is East Seattle which was the original community center of the Island. This planned community was envisioned by C.C. Calkins who bought land starting in 1887 to fulfill his dream of creating a non-industrial, residentially-oriented community. In its heyday, the East Seattle community was reached by ferry, crowned by a lush hotel, and included rental cottages, a few all-year homes, a store, school, Episcopal Church, post office, dance hall and a telephone and an electrical system.

0.1 mi   Half a block down the street on your left you'll see the historic Mercer Island Craft Guild. The Guild was founded in April 1940 during the Great Depression. The Guild allowed Mercer Island residents to share tools and talents to help them complete their homes during the Great Depression. Today, this remarkable community group is still sharing tools and expertise for non-commercial projects.

Continue down 61ˢᵗ. Along the way you can still see some of the buildings built during this period, using the expertise and tools from the Guild.

Turn-by-Turn Directions:

- **Start:** Boys and Girls Club on SE 28ᵗʰ Street and West Mercer Way
- Left on E 28ᵗʰ St (West)
- Left on 61ˢᵗ Ave SE
- Right on SE 32ⁿᵈ Street
- Right on 60ᵗʰ Ave SE
- Right on Lid Park Trail just before I-90 Bridge underpass
- Across West Mercer up northeast Lid Park Trail
- Left at ballparks to 72ⁿᵈ Ave SE
- Left on North Mercer Way
- Right at driveway of #2029 to SE 22ⁿᵈ St Trail
- Left on 60ᵗʰ Ave SE
- Left on SE 24ᵗʰ St
- Right on 61ˢᵗ Ave SE
- Left on SE 27ᵗʰ St
- Through Secret Park to West Mercer Way
- Right on SE 28ᵗʰ St
- **End:** Boys & Girls Club

0.3 mi   **Take a right on 32ⁿᵈ and head down to Proctor Landing.** Notice that some of the homes list their address as Proctor Lane. During the depression, the Federal Works Progress Administration (WPA) was established locally and one of the projects created was the numbering of the streets on Mercer Island. At the time, all of the streets were named—usually family names of the original owner. The Planning Department argued that numbered streets caused less confusion and to the chagrin of the community, the street numbers were aligned with streets in Seattle and communities to the north and south.

0.8 mi   32ⁿᵈ ends at Proctor Landing which was named after some of the first Island residents, Gardiner Proctor and his Native American wife Ellen, who in the 1880's homesteaded 160 acres that reached from the floating bridge south to SE 34ᵗʰ St and from West Mercer Way to the lakeshore. Gardiner Proctor died in 1889 and Ellen returned to her family on the Black River. The site of the old Proctor Cabin was south of SE 32ⁿᵈ formerly known as Lane's Point. The old cabin was destroyed sometime in the 1940's.

Take a right on 60th Ave SE heading past a series of waterfront access points--Garfield Landing, Slater Park and Calkins Landing.

All are pleasant rest stops. Garfield has a nice rock to sit on and put your feet in the water; Slater Park has a table and lawn for a great picnic; and Calkins Landing has some nice shady benches. Slater Park also has an interesting piece of public art—a cast concrete sculpture by Marge Hammond-Farness called "Water-Moss Bowl." Every one of these waterfront access points are great viewing spots for the Blue Angels at SeaFair. It's crowded, loud and very fun.

Stop at Calkins Landing for a peek into history. In the early days, Calkins Landing was known as the East Seattle Dock. Nearby was the very ornate Calkins Hotel—a three story building with wide verandas, towers and a grand staircase. The hotel was at the center of the grand plan of C.C. Calkins who had a vision of turning Mercer Island from wilderness to a resort for fashionable ladies and gentlemen from Seattle. The enterprise thrived for several years, and even hosted President Benjamin Harrison, before personal misfortune, compounded by the depression of 1893 had Calkins leave for an unknown destination, never to return. The property was later used as a home for delinquent boys, a sanitarium and a boarding house, before burning to the ground in 1908.

Although the hotel was destroyed, the East Seattle location remained the center of business on the Island for over 50 years. Only when the floating bridge changed the traffic flow patterns did the business activity move to the current north central business center. The first commercial building on the island was a large structure, built around 1900, located at SE 28th and 60th Ave SE. At street level there was a general store, Mrs. Gilbert's bakery, and the Post Office. On the second floor was a hall for meetings, dances and gatherings. During the 1940's, the store closed and eventually the old building was torn down.

Continue on 60th Ave SE. This street was named Navy Yard Road, until the 1930's, because of thoughts of using Mercer Island as a U.S. Navy Yard. It was rumored that President Lincoln himself pointed to Mercer Island on a map and stated that it would be a good place for a Navy Yard. At the time, the rumor started a land rush, but the Navy Yard was later established in Bremerton.

0.9 mi   **Eventually, 60th Ave SE will pass under I-90. Just prior to passing under the freeway, take the path on your right that leads up to Lid Park on the north side of SE 24th.**

1.2 mi   **At the top of the hill you will reach West Mercer Way and will see Lid Park kitty-corner from the trail. Carefully, cross to your left over the freeway ramp, and then cross again over West Mercer Way to the trail that leads up to the playground.**

You might want to take a break here, and enjoy the beautiful sculptures of the little girl and dog—surprisingly, they were created by different artists. The dog is titled "Playful Pup" and was created by Gary Price, and the girl is titled "Stepping Forward" and was created by Dennis Smith. Both are renowned inspirational artists from Utah.

1.4 mi   **When you're ready, head up the trail to the top of "The Lid".** Officially named "Luther Burbank Lid Park", it's a one-of-a-kind park built on top of a freeway. The park occupies a concrete 'lid' covering a half-mile stretch of I-90 and was completed in 1994. The lid was intended to muffle the noise and reconnect neighborhoods that were severed when the old Sunset Highway became I-90. The park is highly unique. Funding for the project was approved in a 1976 environmental-impact statement and was locked in by a federal court decision, thus protecting it against the government frugality of the 1980's.

Turn around for a minute and you will get a look at the Floating Bridge behind you. Completed in 1940, the original floating bridge was the largest floating structure built by man. It was considered an engineering marvel of the time as no bridge like it had ever been built. The bridge was first proposed as a private enterprise, but the stock market crash of '29 ended those efforts. It later was filed as Docket No 1 on the first Public Works Assistance program. Why a floating bridge? The depth of the lake (more than 200 feet at its deepest), the length of the crossing (1-1/4 miles), and a soft and muddy lake bottom ruled out a conventional bridge. More than 3,000 men were employed for 18 months during construction. The 25 floating concrete sections were built in Harbor Island paving docks and towed through the locks and the ship canal to the bridge site. The original bridge was a two-way, four-lane toll bridge.

Mercer Island resident George Lightfoot was known as the father of the Floating Bridge because of his persistence and dedication to the project. A monument of appreciation to him can be found in Roanoke Park where we will pass later on this walk. The building of the bridge marked the end of an era on Mercer Island—changing the culture from a small rural island to a suburb of Seattle. The original bridge sank in a storm on November 25, 1990 while it was undergoing repair. Our current two newer bridges are now the second and third longest floating bridges with the longest being the Evergreen Floating Bridge, a few miles north across Lake Washington.

1.5 mi **The trail will descend to the baseball field where you should veer left toward the restrooms. There is a drinking fountain here and even a special spot to water your pooch. Continue left out of the park where the trail emerges at SE 72nd. Cross the road and take a right so you are walking against traffic and head down the hill. You will cross SE 20th which offers a short cut to Roanoke Park and a trail back up to the Lid Park, but continue straight.**

1.7 mi Soon you will see the VFW building on your right. The VFW Hall started out as the Keewaydin Club in 1922. North Side residents created this building for social events—parties, dances and meetings—and named it after "the north wind." Later, the building became known as the Mercer Island Community Club where residents met to socialize and discuss the issues of their growing community. In 1966 VFW Post No 5760 bought the building, remodeled it and today continues to rent it out to social and civic groups.

Almost directly across the street you will see the Roanoke Inn. The Roanoke Inn was built by George McGuire in 1914. Originally, a "chicken-dinner' inn that was close to the ferry dock, the inn is still in operation as a tavern and is considered a gem of the island community. McGuire built the Roanoke to take advantage of the growing number of tourists exploring the island by car. Over the years, the business was rumored to have been a brothel and purveyor of illegal booze during the prohibition, and later served groceries, ice cream and pop. In 1943 Mr. and Mrs. Edwin Reeck made the tavern into what it is today, a beloved island meeting place with a warm atmosphere, food and drinks. The Inn has stayed in the family, and is owned and run by Dorothy Reeck today.

We'll take a left on West Mercer Way, but if you continue straight down 72nd you'll find a nice grassy spot with a shady tree, beach access and a view to Bellevue at the 72nd Ave SE Landing.

1.8 mi Just before a little park on your left, you will see Roanoke Way on your right, which leads to Roanoke Landing—where the ferry to Seattle docked from the early 1890's until the floating bridge was built in 1940. First the steamer C.C. Calkins and later the little ferry Dawn, made their way around the Island from dock to dock, providing the main transportation and services for Island residents. There isn't beach access, but it's worth the walk down the lane to take in the gorgeous view toward Leschi in Seattle.

The little park on your left is a hidden neighborhood park, Roanoke Park, with its always-available tennis courts, children's play structure and water fountain.

Continue on West Mercer Way, past the park. At the end you will see a trail sign that will lead you back up to SE 20ᵗʰ and the Lid Park, but you will continue straight.

1.9 mi   Just past two white posts on your left you'll see a road that veers off West Mercer to your right and down a hill. Look for concrete walls, and mailbox numbers #2029 and 2025. Cross West Mercer and go down the road. At the bottom of the dip in the road, stay left on the trail going past a gate on your right. You'll travel along north of I-90 on a little trail with spectacular views all the way up the lake.

2.1 mi   The trail ends at the terminus of 22ⁿᵈ Street in the area named Faban Point. Head down 22ⁿᵈ, and then take a left on 60ᵗʰ past the grand houses of this neighborhood. Pass under I-90, cross the street and then take a left on 24ᵗʰ Street going up the hill, then your first right on 61ˢᵗ Street. At SE 27ᵗʰ take a left and go three blocks to Secret Park.

2.7 mi   At the top of the hill you will see tiny Secret Park on your right. Secret Park is the site of the first school building on Mercer Island. Known as the "Little White Schoolhouse", the building was built in 1890, serving the community for 24 years as a school and community gathering spot until it burned to the ground in 1914. Cut through the Park and see the picnic area and playground . When you're finished at the Park, continue through the Park on the path and you will emerge at SE 28ᵗʰ St and West Mercer Way.

This was the original location of the first church on Mercer Island, the Emmanuel Episcopal Church. The church was started as a mission in 1909 and the small congregation met in a home in East Seattle. In 1914, the church was able to raise funds to build a small, rustic church on what is now West Mercer Way and SE 27ᵗʰ. Later a Guild Hall was added east of the church almost next to East Seattle School. Soon the Church and Guild had become a key aspect of the social fabric of East Seattle—prompting an old timer to explain that "everyone was an Episcopalian in those days." The Emmanuel Episcopal Church on Mercer Island is still going strong, after more than 100 years, at its relatively new location in the Maple Lane neighborhood near the library.

2.8 mi   The walk ends back at the Boys and Girls Club. Island 'old timers' know the Boys and Girls Club as East Seattle School. The activity area of the club was built in 1914 and was a school for almost 100 Island students. The main entrance for the school was originally on the west side of the terra cotta colored building. In 1938 a federal grant allowed the addition of a gymnasium and auditorium to the school. Labor was provided through a Works Progress Administration Program, and recycled lumber from two closed schools (Barnabie and Allview Heights) was used. By 1941 all students on the Island went to school here until 1950, when population growth fueled the creation of our current schools. The building continued as a school until the mid 1970's when it was leased and later sold to the Boys and Girls Club. The fate of the building is now in question with the approval of the new Boys and Girls "PEAK" project. The building is likely to be torn down in the next year or so to make way for ball fields.

"All truly great thoughts are conceived while walking."
Fredrich Nietzsche

Moderate Walk |
North End Parks Loop

The North End Park Loop connects the big North End public parks in a pleasant 3.6 mile loop. The walk starts at Lid Park, takes you through Luther Burbank Park, through the Outdoor Sculpture Gallery and back. Most of the walk is on either paved roads or paths, and the slopes are relatively gentle. Bring money for a coffee or smoothie along the way as you'll skirt the North End of town.

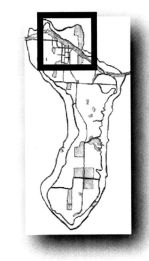

Rating: Moderate

Length: 3.6 miles

Terrain: Mostly paved park trails, quiet residential streets, some dirt trails.

Highlights: Wide open parks, beautiful views.

Trailhead: Start at Lid Park near the baseball fields off of 74th Ave SE

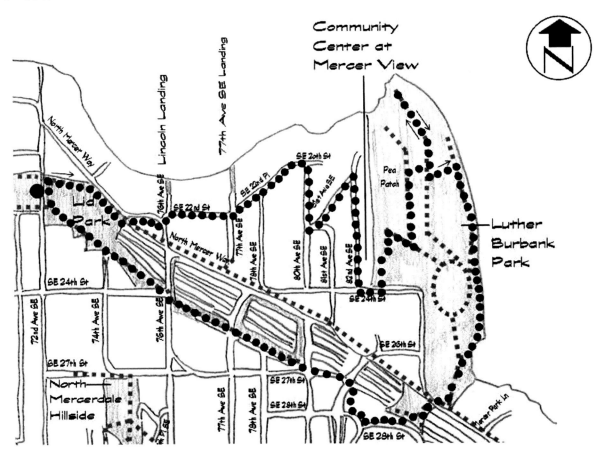

Guided Tour: North End Parks Loop

0.0 mi Start at the baseball fields at Lid Park. From the parking lot enter the Park from the north, near the restrooms. Take the trail that goes off to the left (northeast). The trail will head around the outfield of the baseball field and will cut down onto a path on the north, below the grassy area of the park.

0.1 mi Stay on the trail at the split—heading right and continuing down.

The trail will parallel North Mercer Way. Be on the lookout for bikes as this is part of the I-90 trail and they really speed through here! On this type of path, always stay to your right. The bikes will pass you on your left and usually will give a verbal warning.

0.3 mi At the corner of 76th Ave SE, and North Mercer Way, cross to your left and then cross North Mercer, going down 76th Ave SE.

You will head down into the neighborhood historically known as McGilvra. Gordon McGilvra platted the area from the waterfront to 32nd Street in 1905. This area was bustling in the early 1900's—having a school and many year-round residents. The McGilvra Improvement Club was started by a group of 21 women in 1914, raising money and volunteering to improve the quality of their lives.

On your left you'll see Lincoln Landing, one of many public water access spots on the Island. This was the site of the McGilva Dock in the early 1900's. The cove on the left has been in the paper as of late regarding an effort to name it. In fact, the early residents of McGilva had a name for the cove—in those days it was known as Serena Cove.

0.4 mi A few blocks further you'll see a second landing on the left—77th Ave SE Landing. Down the path, you will find a great view with a bench shaded by a wonderful old cedar tree. Take the time for a quick peek.

Turn-by-Turn Directions:

- **Start:** Lid Park Ballpark, off 74th Ave SE
- South on northern Lid Park Trail
- Left at trail split
- At 76th Ave SE Cross and go down 76th Ave SE
- Continue on SE 22nd St
- Right on 80th Ave SE
- Left on SE 22nd St
- Right on 82nd Ave SE
- Left at SE 24th St
- Left at Community Center
- Straight on path to Pea Patch
- Right at Pea Patch down trail
- Left at gravel pathway
- Retrace steps then left after Off-Leash Dog area
- Right at path along water
- Left on path at beach toward parking lot
- Exit parking lot
- Left on North Mercer Way
- Cross NMW at crosswalk & go right on I-90 Trail.
- Left up freeway overpass
- Right at 'T' in the path
- Cross Island Crest Way, then cross again at SE 27th St
- Path behind Tully's to Sculpture Park
- Cross 24th and go up the path to Lid Park
- **End:** Lid Park Ballpark

0.6 mi   Continue along SE 22ⁿᵈ until you reach 80ᵗʰ Ave SE and then take a right up the hill. Take a left on SE 22ⁿᵈ and then another quick left on SE 81ˢᵗ Ave SE, continuing up.

0.9 mi   At the top of the hill take a right on 82ⁿᵈ Ave SE. Town Center is on your left and you'll get a great view of Seattle here. Head down the hill and take a left at the stop sign on SE 24ᵗʰ St.

1.1 mi   Soon you will come to the parking lot for the Community Center at Mercerview. Take a left at the first parking lot driveway and head toward the hill just left of the Community Center.

In 1960, during a period of significant growth, this property housed an elementary school called Mercer View. The school was closed in June, 1980 and leased to the city for the Community Center. The building was demolished and rebuilt in 2004. If you need a drink of water or use the restrooms, this is a good spot. The Community Center almost always houses an art show which is fun to pop in and see.

Behind the brick shed you will see a gravel path that heads up the hill. Before heading up, you might want to check out the beautiful bronze sculpture of a horse. This is called "Peruvian Paso Colt" and was created by the late John Halko, best known for his wildlife sculpture.

1.3 mi   As you continue up the gravel path, you will see a path down to the small Community Center building below. Stay to the left and continue up the hill to the Pea Patch.

The community Pea Patch offers a place to garden for residents who lack space. The Patch is popular and the previous year's gardeners have priority; so you'll need to get on the waiting list through the Community Center if you're interested in joining the fun. The Pea Patch is really fun to visit from April to October as the place is bustling with those with a green thumb. Just be sure to respect the work of the gardeners by keeping the kids and dogs out of the gardens.

Continue along the path at the bottom of the Pea Patch, and take in the gorgeous views. Then, just before the shed take a right and carefully head down the bark path to Luther Burbank Park. This area is thick with blackberries during the late summer—so build in some time in case you need to have a little snack—Yum!

1.4 mi   At the bottom of the trail, you'll see the Luther Burbank parking lot on your right. Take a left on the gravel pathway that leads off the parking lot, heading north. You'll meander along the northwest end of the Park, passing the amphitheater on your right.

Luther Burbank Park is a 77 acre park with .75 miles of waterfront. The Park has a public boat dock, fishing pier, swimming beach, amphitheater, tennis courts, picnic areas and a popular off-leash dog area, complete with access to the lake. The Park has been owned by the City of Mercer Island since 2003, when it took over its maintenance from King County who had purchased the park land in 1969.

The park land was originally homesteaded in 1887 by Charles Calkins who founded East Seattle—the original commercial center of the Island in the late 1800's. His family home was located at the northern most point of the Park. He lived there until he left the Island due to personal tragedy and the 1893 depression.

In 1901, the School Board in Seattle bought the Calkins Homestead for a Boys Parental School—a school for children who needed care—creating a program of farm work and study that lasted on the Island for 36 years. The school was a self-sufficient farm of more than 100 acres, with the boys learning farm work and assisting with every aspect of running the farm. You can still see some remains of the farming operation and buildings in the Park.

The Park is named after the famous horticulturist—Luther Burbank—who is credited with developing hybridized plants, grafted trees, the baking potato, and many flowers. Ironically, he also created the Himalya Blackberry, which in places chokes the Park's native vegetation—but sure taste good.

1.5 mi   On your left you will see a raised trail through the North Wetlands. The wildlife that you might see is worth the short trip out to the viewpoint at the end, and there is a great hidden picnic table along the way. You might see and hear herons, red winged blackbirds, frogs—even some turtles on the rocks. From the point at the end you can see a beaver dam—and maybe see beavers busy at work. As you walk to the point, notice the little trees they have felled.

1.6 mi   **Continuing down the gravel path, you will see the Off-Leash Dog Area on your right and the remains of the stables of the Boys School that used to be here. Continue on the path, and head out for the spectacular view from the North End of the Park.** This viewpoint is Calkins Point, and the location of the Calkins home in the late 1800's. No wonder he came to Mercer Island!

1.7 mi   **Return to the stables the way you came, and then take the paved path on your left that goes past the Off-Leash Dog Area and toward the large brick building and playground.**

1.8 mi   **Just after the dog area, take a left on the gravel path that winds down toward the water. Then take a right on the path that skirts the waterfront.**

Again, you'll see the affects of beavers on the Alders! On your right, the brick building which now houses the City of Mercer Island Parks and Recreation Department was built in 1929 as the dormitory for the Boys Parental School.

2.0 mi   Soon you will come to another old building—the boiler building—which was also a part of the school farm operation, but now is the central site for boating lessons on the Island. Notice the beautiful artwork on the chain fence simply called "Hands." The dock is public and rarely busy.

If you take the path up to your right, you will come to the children's playground, but for this walk we'll continue along the waterfront on the woodchip path.

2.2 mi   The trail gets a little rustic along here, but the quiet it provides is lovely. Along the way, you will see another dock—used even less than the others—a good quiet place for enjoying a little sun on a nice day.

2.3 mi   **Eventually, you'll emerge at a daisy covered hill above the swimming beach—a wonderful place for kids to swim—and you'll meet up with a path. Take the leftmost branch of the path, heading toward the crazy looking grass hills above.**

2.4 mi   Called "The Source" these mounds are one of the best earthform artworks in the region. Created by John Hope, this piece has three circular mounds covered with grass that radiate around a granite fountain. The water gently flows from the central fountain and runs along a shallow gully lined with smooth round rocks into Lake Washington. It's a living artwork and a favorite of kids of all sizes and ages. First you go up a hill and pretty soon you're running all over the place. Go ahead, explore it a bit! It's very infectious.

When you're finished, take a left and head past another marsh, more blackberries, and the lower parking lot.

2.5 mi   At the parking lot, take a right up to 84th Ave SE where you'll emerge at 26th St, then a left on 84th Ave. Walk until you reach the crosswalk, cross over to the multiuse path and take a right, back the way you came. Again, remember to stay to your right and watch out for those fast moving bikes!

2.7 mi   At the top of the rise, you'll see a freeway overpass on your left. Take a left up the overpass, stopping at the viewpoint at the top—gorgeous! This brings you to an area of the Park that many Islanders don't know exists. This little used spot has a large grass area, perfect—in my opinion—for a Frisbee Football game! Okay, it's a little loud with the freeway noise, but otherwise, lovely. The sculpture of the eagle on your right is called 'Mercy'. The piece was created by Sara Malljohani who said this about her artwork:

"The bald eagle is America's symbol of pride and glory, sacred to the Native People and later adopted by the new Americans. Our compassion, our mercy has brought it back from the edge of extinction to which we drove it. Can we also commit our energy to the recovery of the wild Northwest and salmon who we have driven to the same precipice? We are all related."

3.0 mi   When you get to the T in the path, go right. Cross Island Crest Blvd, then cross again at SE 27th Street, then one more time so that you are next to the colorful sculpture. This sculpture is called "Primavera II" and was created by internationally known artist Roslyn Mazzilli who was born in New York in 1941 and now has a studio in California. She says that in this piece she was trying to show in an abstract way, the outstretched wings of a bird—about to land or balanced and hovering. Many of her sculptures show movement in natural happenings.

Continue on the path (to the right of Tully's) into the wonderful Outdoor Sculpture Gallery. Enjoy the works that are displayed here on a rotating basis. All of the pieces shown are for sale.

3.2 mi   At the end of the Gallery, you'll see the Mercer Island "Gateway" artwork. The whimsical people just kind of make me giggle—I just love them. They were created by Garth Edwards from Bainbridge Island out of powdered coated steel.

Cross 77th and continue on the path. This area was the old Sunset Highway—the first road across Mercer Island and the center of town after the bridge was built in 1940. It looks very different now with our tall multi-use buildings!

3.3 mi   Cross 24th at the second crossing and head for the path up the hill back into Lid Park.

Officially named, Luther Burbank Lid Park, this park is a one-of-a-kind park built on top of a freeway. The Park occupies a concrete lid covering a half-mile stretch of I-90 and was completed in 1994. The lid was intended to muffle the noise and reconnect neighborhoods that were severed when the old Sunset Highway became I-90. The Park is highly unique. Funding for the project was approved in the 1976 environmental-impact statement and was locked in by a federal court decision, thus protecting it against the government frugality of the 1980's.

3.6 mi   You will pass the playground and a covered area (which is available for rent) on your right, and then a great sculpture by Mark Heisel entitled 'Hope.' The artist tells us this sculpture is meant to represent the spirit of energy that runs through us and surrounds us as individuals. He believes that it is that same spirit or energy that connects us to those around us and to the whole earth and everything in it. We thank the Silverman Family for placing it there in remembrance and for the enjoyment of all of us.

Then continue up past the ballpark to your original starting point.

"In every walk with nature one receives far more than he seeks."
John Muir

Ambitious Walk |
History Loop and Hillclimb

This walk has it all—historical sites, dramatic homes, big hills, huge views, deep woods, and many Mercer Island hidden treasures. It is for the fairly hardy, as the hike starts and ends with lots of stairs, with plenty of fast-paced paved walking in between. Bring some money along as there are opportunities to stop for lunch, a drink or a snack along the way. Also, this is a great hike during SeaFair as it allows you to park in town and walk to where the Blue Angels will fly directly overhead.

Rating:	Ambitious
Length:	3.5 miles
Terrain:	Steep wooded stairs, quiet residential streets and paths.
Highlights:	Historical sites, impressive homes, huge waterfront views
Trailhead:	Start at Bicentennial Park, corner of 77th Ave SE and SE 32nd St

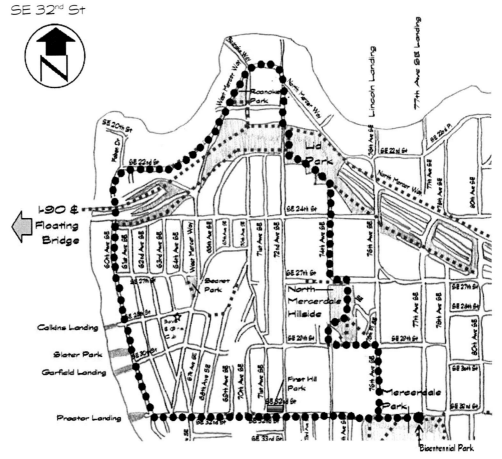

Guided Walk: History Loop & Hillclimb

0.0 mi   Start at Bicentennial Park using the park bathrooms if needed. Looking up the hill, you'll see the start of the stairs leading up into the woods. Head straight up the stairs, being careful on the slippery wood in wet weather.

You are heading up the north edge of Mercerdale Park which connects to Mercerdale Hillside Park to the south. Now a quiet respite and home to some of our favorite Mercer Island events, the Mercerdale Park property has had a lively history over the years. Starting out as a swamp, it was later leveled and became prime real estate as Island happenings moved to the Central District. In 1956 the property was bought by the school district to serve as a school site, but was not needed as school enrollment declined. The City later acquired the parcel, trading the current City Hall building for it, and plans were underway to develop the area as a Civic Center. Many opposed the idea and it was put to a vote in 1987. Voters narrowly defeated the idea; properties were swapped again and the current 9611 City Hall building was renovated.

0.1 mi   At the first junction, continue up—the trail on your left leads back down to Mercerdale Hillside Park—a good walk to take another day.

Above Sunrise Assisted Living you will see another set of stairs, this time on the right—our loop will bring us back here later, but for now, continue on up veering left.

0.2 mi   The third junction has a trail to the left which also leads to Mercerdale Hillside Park—again, continue up.

0.3 mi   The top of the stairs will emerge at the corner of SE 32nd St and 74th Place SE and you will crest the hill at 74th Ave SE in the heart of the First Hill neighborhood. After you peek behind you for a view of town far below, continue straight along SE 32nd Street.

The lot on your right is surplus city land. As you can imagine, there are many differing opinions on its future use being debated at City Council meetings. The First Hill neighborhood is a mix of the old and the new. Over the last 5 years, these smaller, more affordable homes with large yards have been a target for tear-down projects causing much controversy and discussion on the Island.

Turn-by-Turn Directions:

- **Start:** Bicentennial Park
- Head up trail on stairs
- Straight at first junction
- Veer left at second junction
- Straight at third junction
- Straight on 32nd
- Straight on path
- Right on 60th Ave
- Under bridge
- Right on SE 22nd
- Continue straight at trail
- Left on West Mercer
- Right on 72nd Ave SE
- Left into Lid Park
- Past ball fields and left towards playground
- Right on 74th Ave SE
- Left on SE 27th
- Right on trail
- Right at junction
- Left down stairs
- **End:** Bicentennial Park

0.4 mi   On the corner of 72nd Ave SE, you will see tiny First Hill Park—a lovely little neighborhood park with wooded slides, a play structure and a small grassy area. Continue over the hill, and down the other side on **SE 32ⁿᵈ Street**—taking in the beautiful views toward **Seward Park.** Enjoy the old vegetation along this road. In the early spring, the camellias are amazing.

0.5 mi   At the end of 32ⁿᵈ at 69ᵗʰ you'll come to a white guard rail. The road ends, but the stairs continue down and meet again at SE 32ⁿᵈ St about two blocks below. Along the way down, you will cross 68ᵗʰ St which, if you go right, has a path that will take you back up to First Hill. For this walk though, continue down the hill and carefully cross West Mercer Way, entering the oldest neighborhood on the Island, East Seattle.

This 'planned' community was envisioned by C.C. Calkins who bought land starting in 1887 to fulfill his dream of creating a non-industrial, residentially-oriented community. In its heyday, the East Seattle community was reached by ferry, crowned by a lush hotel, and included rental cottages, a few all-year homes, a store, school, Episcopal Church, post office, dance hall and a telephone and electrical system.

0.7 mi   Along the way, you'll cross 61ˢᵗ Ave SE. It might be worth the 1 ½ block detour to the right on 61ˢᵗ Ave SE to see the historic Mercer Island Craft Guild. The Guild was founded in April 1940 during the great depression. The Guild allowed Mercer Island residents to share tools and talents to help them complete their homes during the great depression. This remarkable community group is still sharing tools and expertise for non-commercial projects today. If you detoured, return to 32ⁿᵈ and head toward the water.

0.8 mi   **SE 32ⁿᵈ ends at Proctor Landing.** The waterfront access point was named after some of the first Island residents, Gardiner Proctor and his Native American wife Ellen, who in the 1880's homesteaded 160 acres that resided from the floating bridge south to SE 34ᵗʰ St and from West Mercer Way to the lakeshore. Gardiner Proctor died in 1889 and Ellen returned to her family on the Black River. The site of the old Proctor Cabin, formerly known as Lane's Point, was just south of SE 32ⁿᵈ. The old cabin was destroyed sometime in the 1940's.

Take a right on 60ᵗʰ Ave SE heading past a series of waterfront access points--Garfield Landing, Slater Park and Calkins Landing. All are pleasant rest stops. Garfield has a nice rock to sit on and put your feet in the water; Slater Park has a table and lawn for a great picnic; and Calkins Landing has some nice shady benches. Slater Park also has an interesting piece of public art—a cast concrete sculpture by Marge Hammond-Farness called "Water-Moss Bowl."

You might want to stop at Calkins Landing for a peek into history. In the early days, Calkins Landing was known as the East Seattle Dock. Nearby was the very ornate Calkins Hotel—a three story structure with wide verandas, towers and a grand staircase. The hotel was at the center of the grand plan of C.C. Calkins who had a vision of turning Mercer Island from wilderness to a resort for fashionable ladies and gentlemen from Seattle. The enterprise thrived for several years, and even hosted President Benjamin Harrison, before personal misfortune, compounded by the depression of 1893 had Calkins leave for an unknown destination never to return. The property was later used as a home for delinquent boys, a sanitarium and a boarding house before burning to the ground in 1908.

Although the hotel was destroyed, the East Seattle location remained the center of business on the island for over 50 years. Only when the floating bridge changed the traffic flow patterns did the business activity move to the current north central business center. The first commercial building on the Island was a large building, built around 1900 that was located at SE 28ᵗʰ and 60ᵗʰ Ave SE. At street level there was a general store, Mrs. Gilbert's Bakery, and the Post Office. On the second floor was a hall for meetings, dances and gatherings. During the 1940's, the store closed and eventually the old building was torn down.

Continue on 60ᵗʰ Ave SE. This street was named Navy Yard Road until the 1930's because of thoughts of using Mercer Island as a U.S. Navy Yard. It was rumored that President Lincoln himself pointed to Mercer Island on a map and stated that it would be a good place for a navy yard.

1.5 mi   **Eventually, 60ᵗʰ Ave SE will pass under I-90—the "floating bridge."**

Completed in 1940, the original floating bridge was the largest floating structure built by man and was considered an engineering marvel of the time as no bridge like it had ever been built. The bridge was first proposed as a private enterprise, but the stock market crash of '29 ended those efforts. It later was filed as docket No 1 on the first Public Works Assistance Program.

Why a floating bridge? The depth of the lake (more than 200 feet at its deepest), the length of the crossing (1-1/4 miles), and a soft and muddy lake bottom ruled out a conventional bridge. During construction, more than 3,000 men were employed for 18 months. The 25 floating concrete sections were constructed in Harbor Island paving docks and towed through the locks and the ship canal to the bridge site. The original was a two-way, four-lane toll bridge.

Mercer Island resident George Lightfoot was known as the father of the Floating Bridge, being extremely very persistent and dedicated to the project. A monument of appreciation to him can be found just up the road in Roanoke Park. The building of the bridge marked the end of an era on Mercer Island—changing the culture from a small rural island to a suburb of Seattle. The original bridge sank in spectacular fashion in a storm on November 25, 1990 while it was undergoing repair.

There are two trails on the right that lead up to Lid Park, but continue along 60ᵗʰ Ave SE into the dramatic Faben Point area of the Island. At SE 22ⁿᵈ St, take a right and you'll find a trail at the end of the road.

1.8 mi   **The trail leads through to West Mercer Way with spectacular views along the way, allowing you to see all the way to the 520 bridge. At the end of the path, continue to West Mercer.** The Evergreen Bridge or 520 is now the longest floating structure in the world—narrowly beating out the two floating I-90 bridges.

2.0 mi   **At West Mercer, you'll see a path to your right that will lead to Lid Park. We'll, however, take a left on West Mercer to the North End of the Island. Soon, on your right you will come to a trail marker. Following the path sign will lead once again to Lid Park, but continue along West Mercer Way.**

On your right will be a hidden neighborhood park, Roanoke Park, with its always-available tennis courts, children's play structure and fountain. (And the location of that monument to Lightfoot!)

2.1 mi   Just after the little park, you will see Roanoke Way on your left which leads to Roanoke Landing—where the ferry to Seattle docked, from the early 1890's until the floating bridge was built in 1940. First the steamer C.C. Calkins and later the little ferry Dawn, made their way around the Island from dock to dock, providing the main transportation for Island residents. There isn't beach access here, but it's worth the walk down Roanoke Way to take in the gorgeous view toward Leschi in Seattle.

2.2 mi   **We'll turn right on 72ⁿᵈ Ave SE, although there is a nice grassy spot with a shady tree and a view to Bellevue if you go ½ a block to the left to the 72ⁿᵈ Ave SE Landing.** Once on 72ⁿᵈ on your right you'll see the jewel of Mercer Island—the Roanoke Inn. If you don't have kids with you, pop in for a snack or a soda, or come back later for a beer. The Inn is a Mercer Island classic.

The Roanoke Inn was built by George McGuire in 1914. Originally, a "chicken-dinner" Inn that was close to the ferry dock, the Inn is still in operation as a tavern and is considered a gem of the island community. McGuire built the Roanoke to take advantage of the growing number of touristreets exploring the Island by car. Over the years, the business was rumored to have been a brothel and purveyor of illegal booze during the prohibition, and later served groceries, ice cream and pop. In 1943 Mr. and Mrs. Edwin Reeck made it into what it is today, a beloved Island meeting place with a warm atmosphere, food and drinks. The Inn has stayed in the family, and is owned and run by Dorthoy Reeck today.

2.3 mi   On your left is the also historic VFW building. The VFW Hall started its life as the Keewaydin Club in 1922. North End residents created this building for social events—parties, dances and meetings—and built the building naming it after "the north wind." Later, the building became known as the Mercer Island Community Club where residents met to socialize and discuss the issues of their growing community. In 1966 VFW Post No 5760 bought the building, remodeled it and continue to rent it out today to social and civic groups.

2.4 mi   **Continue up the hill and just before the bridge, duck into the Lid Park through the pathway on your left. Here you'll find bathrooms if you feel the need. Take a right at Fereglia Fields, and then a left behind the dugout staying on the main trail so that you're headed down toward the covered shelter and playground.**

Officially named "Luther Burbank Lid Park", this park is one-of-a-kind built on top of a freeway. The park occupies a concrete 'lid' covering a half-mile stretch of I-90 and was completed in 1994. The lid was intended to muffle the noise and reconnect neighborhoods that were severed when the old Sunset Highway became I-90. The park is highly unique. Funding for the project was approved in a 1976 environmental-impact statement and was locked in by a federal court decision, thus protecting it against the government frugality of the 1980's.

2.5 mi   On your left you will see a beautiful sculpture by Mark Heisel entitled 'Hope.' The artist tells us this sculpture is meant to represent the spirit of energy that runs through us and surrounds us as individuals. He believes that it is that same spirit or energy that connects us to those around us and to the whole earth and everything in it. We thank the Silverman Family for placing it there in remembrance and for the enjoyment of all of us.

This path continues all the way down to Sculpture Park, but we're going to take a right just past the field on the path that leads to the end of 74th Ave SE.

2.75 mi   **Follow 74th and cross busy SE 24th St with care, dipping down and back up again to the North Mercerdale Hillside Park. Skip the first entrance to the Park as it takes you back up to First Hill exiting at 27th & 74th.**

2.85 mi   **Take the second entrance on your right just above the complex that houses the Islander Restaurant (where kids are welcome.) You'll walk under the trees and through millions of ferns. Skip the stairs on the right that lead up to First Hill, continuing straight. At the parking lot take the stairs to the right. The trail will lead down to the corner of 76th and 29th**

3.15 mi   **Take a right on 76th and walk along the road and up the driveway of the Sunrise Assisted Living facility.**

3.30 mi   **At the end of the driveway, go up the stairs, taking a left at the junction. You will be back on the original starting trail that heads down to Bicentennial Park. Head down the hill staying left at the junction.**

3.5 mi   **End at Bicentennial Park.**

"I walk slowly, but I never walk backward."
Abraham Lincoln

Family Walk |
Pond, Park and Library

The gem of this walk is the darling natural pond full of ducks along the way. It starts at the library, so bring your library card to check out a book about ponds and their inhabitants or plants of the area. Some gorgeous, old native plants can be seen along the way. The walk ends at the highest elevation on Mercer Island—Rotary Park. This walk is great with kids—even in a stroller or on their bikes or scooters. Also one to remember for the first winter snow—it's nice and flat—great for towing a sled—and nice and quiet.

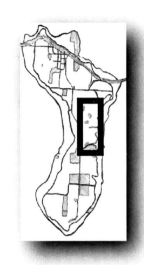

Rating: Family

Length: 1.6 miles

Terrain: Quiet residential streets, and paved & dirt paths.

Highlights: Ducks, library, old native plant species.

Trailhead: Start at the Library at 88th Ave SE and SE 44th St

Guided Tour: Pond, Park and Library

0.0 mi   Start at the Mercer Island Library at 4400 88th Ave SE. From the parking lot, take a left on 88th Ave SE, heading south.

The Mercer Island Library is located at the site of the second school on Mercer Island, Allview Heights School, which was built in 1890 on land donated by Vitus Schmid. The Schmid family—some of the Island's first residents--pioneered the Maple Lane area. Lack of roads made travel to the Little White Schoolhouse in East Seattle impossible for some families, so a local school house was built. The school was closed in 1895 for lack of students and torn down in 1938 with the lumber being used to build the gymnasium at East Seattle School. In the 1950's the land was transferred by the school board to the library board and the library was opened here in 1955.

0.1 mi   **Take left on SE 45th Street**

At the corner of 90th Ave SE, you can peek into the Hollerbach Open Space area—at 5.18 acres, it's one of several unimproved open space areas owned by the City.

0.2 mi   **Go right on 90th Ave SE.**

This quiet street has some wonderful old foliage from by-gone days. People in this neighborhood seem to enjoy their yards. There are some enviable vegetable gardens along here, and a great yard with some wonderful old fruit trees—including apple and cherries—and a huge plum tree.

0.3 mi   **The road ends at Ellis Pond.**

Ellis Pond is a natural pond tucked between homes on the top of the Island. Many bird and animal species can be found in this lovely four-acre pond habitat. Ellis Pond is a product of the care provided by the community that surrounds it. Local neighbors have planted native trees and shrubs and been great stewards for the park.

Turn-by-Turn Directions:

- **Start:** Mercer Island Library
- Left on 88th
- Left on SE 45th
- Right on 90th
- Left across raised walkway
- Right on 91st
- Right on 48th and curving right to trail
- Cross 47th heading straight on 89th
- Left on trail across from Ellis Pond
- Cross 88th, continuing on 46th
- Left at SE 45th
- Right on 86th
- Right on 44th
- Right on 45th
- **End:** Mercer Island Library

When you are done hanging out with the ducks, take a left across the raised walkway, enjoying the fruits of the neighborhood native plant restoration efforts. Then take a right on 91st Avenue.

0.5 mi   At 47th Street, you'll see some pillars on your left. These mark the top of the 47th Street Open Space, a 1 ½ acre area that runs between here and East Mercer Way—another one of those unimproved city-owned areas. As it stands, there are no official cut-thrus between East Mercer and the middle of the Island from the Shoreclub to 53rd SE. Wouldn't this be a perfect one?

The home at #4744 must be home to an artist—there's always something fun to see in this yard—a cool log mailbox post made into a dog, a wire body form, an alien on a pillar...you never know what you'll find here!

0.6 mi   **Take a right on 48th Street, crossing 90th. At the curve in the road, you'll see a cut-thru to Island Crest Way—we'll continue curving right, staying on the paved road. At the end of the road, take the path that cuts-thru to 47th Street.**

0.8 mi   **Cross 47th, heading straight on 89th.**

1.0 mi   **You'll see two trails on your right that head back to Ellis Pond. Across from the second one, take a left on the path, going away from the Pond. Continue straight across 88th, continuing on 46th Street. If you take a left at 87th, you'll find another cut-thru to Island Crest Way, but we'll take a right today.**

1.3 mi   **At SE 45th, take a left and then a right on 86th Avenue SE—skirting the property of Emmanuel Episcopal Church—complete with garden and old fruit trees.** A cherry orchard known as Melhorn Orchard was located on this block-square tract of land originally homesteaded by the Schmid family. Emmanuel Church purchased the property when it sought parish status in 1955 after a long history on the Island. Emmanuel was the first church on Mercer Island. The Church was started as a mission in 1909 and the small congregation met in a home in East Seattle. In 1914, the parishioners were able to raise funds to build a small, rustic church on what is now West Mercer Way and SE 27th and later a Guild Hall was added east of the Church almost next to the Boys and Girls Club. Soon the Church and Guild had become a key aspect of the social fabric of East Seattle—prompting an old timer to explain that "everyone was an Episcopalian in those days." The Emmanuel Episcopal Church on Mercer Island is still going strong after more than 100 years here in its relatively new location.

1.4 mi   **You'll see Maple Lane on your left, and then we'll take a right on 44th.**

              The Maple Lane area was homesteaded in the late 1800's by Vitus Schmid, a wagon-maker's apprentice from Baden, Germany. He and John Wensler, a cobbler from Chicago, filed a 160 acre claim on this part of the island and built a cabin here in 1876. Schmid and Wensler left after a tree fell on their hand-built cabin, but Schmid returned with a wife and family in 1978—filing a new claim. His cabin was here—in the area now known as Maple Lane—until 1954 when it was torn down to make way for modern houses.

1.5 mi   **At the top of the hill you'll see Rotary Park—the highest elevation on Mercer Island.**

              Rotary Park began in 1970 as a Rotary Club project and has since evolved into a neighborhood park. It's the highest elevation on the Island and is home to the City's water storage facility. Trails loop the towers and lead into the neighborhoods behind the park.

1.6 mi   **Take a right on 45th and you'll find the entrance to the Library again.**

              Before you go, don't forget to take in the great sculpture in front of the library, which Islander's love. Titled "Between Two Worlds," this bronze sculpture depicts a boy lying against an impossibly huge rabbit, reading a book with an identical, but life-size rabbit nearby. The artist, Georgia Gerber, wanted the piece to encourage involvement—inviting children to climb on the piece and read along with the boy. Many times I've picked up my daughter to find her reading her new library books atop the rabbits back or sitting right next to the boy. The piece certainly speaks to the "ability of the written word to free the imagination."

"In the beginning you must subject yourself to the influence of nature. You must be able to walk firmly on the ground before you start walking on a tightrope."
Henri Matisse

Family Walk |
53ʳᵈ and Parkwood Ridge Climb

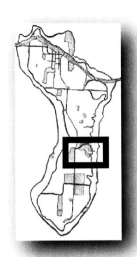

This 1.4 mile loop explores the SE 53ʳᵈ and Parkwood Ridge Open Space areas in one connected loop. Both trail systems are relatively new, so they are well maintained and in good condition even in the wet winter months. This walk is a great in the morning because there is little traffic on the short section that goes along East Mercer Way that time of day. Also, in the early morning, I regularly see owls in the trees through here, so keep a sharp eye. Although relatively short, this hilly climb is guaranteed to get your heart rate up. The directions follow a clock-wise course, but it's a whole new hike the other direction; so try it both ways!

Rating: Family
Length: 1.4 miles
Terrain: Forested paths, some residential streets.
Highlights: Beautiful forests, tree-top bird watching and owls early in the morning.
Trailhead: Start at 53ʳᵈ Open Space at 53ʳᵈ Place SE and East Mercer Way

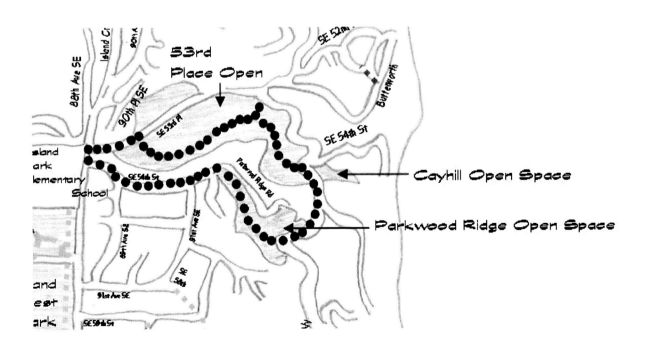

Guided Walk: 53rd & Parkwood Ridge Climb

0.0 mi   **From the SE 53rd Open Space trailhead sign on East Mercer Way and 53rd Place SE, head up and into the woods.**

The 25 acres of wooded SE 53rd Place Open Space was originally purchased in 1989 with a King Country Parks and Open Space Bond Issue and grant funds from the Washington State Interagency Committee for Outdoor Recreation. In the Fall of 2006, a new trail system was unveiled that connects two points along East Mercer Way and one at the top of SE 53rd Place. The trail was the result of a partnership between the City of Mercer Island and the Mountains to Sound Greenway Trust. In fact, Eagle Scouts from several of the Boy Scout troops on Mercer Island did much of the trail completion work.

On your way up you'll soon leave the neighborhood and disappear into a true forest, coming to a large stump on your right with a healthy huckleberry bush growing from it. The log is most likely a remnant of the logging period. Mercer Island was logged of its old growth forest by the turn of the century, so the trees you see were either small saplings during the harvest, or second growth. As you head up the trail, you'll notice very large maples and alders that make up the majority of this forest—very different from Pioneer Park's cedars, hemlocks and firs. Further up you'll see stumps that have nursed new trees—with roots that have grown down over the trunk, even as the trunk has eroded.

You'll also notice a large number of trees entwined with dead ivy or supporting scars of ivy removal. Since the summer of 2005, volunteer ivy-removal groups have spent hours cutting "survival rings" around trees to kill the ivy and prevent it from killing the trees and then pulling the ivy from the tree. This step is part of a multi-year project to improve the ecological health of this natural ravine.

Turn-by-Turn Directions:

- **Start:** East Mercer Wy & 53rd Pl
- Take trail
- Left at junction
- Emerge at East Mercer Way and go right
- At Parkwood Ridge Trail sign, take a right.
- Take Parkwood Ridge to top of hill
- Continue on 54th SE
- Right at Island Crest Way
- Right on 53rd Place SE
- Right on trail into 53rd Place Open Space
- Left at junction
- **End:** East Mercer Way & 53rd PlSE

0.1 mi   **At the trail junction, take a left.**

In the spring, this area is filled with trillium—the three leafed flower that has special meaning to those in the Northwest. They are worth a special outing into the woods—but please don't pick them—they won't grow back next year if they are picked.

0.2 mi   **You'll continue up and over a little hill where the sun pokes through, allowing wildflowers to grow in the spring.**

On your left at the bend, you'll see a twin set of trees that are again growing out of an old stump. Here you're high above East Mercer Way—bypassing cars and bikes in a pocket of quiet. Along here, I love the conifers with ferns growing out of them. Also, along this trail, you might see milk cartons lying on the ground. Don't worry—they aren't litter. They are a mechanism for getting water to new plantings, so you can leave them be.

0.3 mi   **Soon, you'll turn a big corner and head down the hill, appearing in the 5400 block of East Mercer Way at a trail sign. Cross East Mercer Way and take a right going south on the road against traffic.**

The ravine on your left here is undeveloped Mercer Island open space called Cayhill Open Space.

0.4 mi   **You'll travel a ¼ mile south on East Mercer, passing the Glenhaven neighborhood on your left and then get a little treat of a view of the East Channel of Lake Washington—the narrow passage between Mercer Island and Bellevue/Renton.**

Just after the big curve, you'll see a large ravine behind a guard rail where the storms of 1997 made a mess of this section of road—causing a large portion of it to slide.

0.5 mi   **Just after the ravine, you'll see on your right the trail sign for Parkwood Ridge Open Space. Cross the road and head up the trail here.**

Be sure to stay on the trail as you're crossing private property here. Parkwood Ridge Open Space is a 3.8 naturally wooded parcel that connects East Mercer Way with the Parkwood neighborhood above. This new trail was opened in 2007, with a local Boy Scout achieving his Eagle Scout Award by coordinating with the Parks Natural Resources Coordinator on slope stabilization and re-vegetation efforts along several sections of the new trail. Over 100 native trees were installed throughout the Open Space during the project.

The forest here is more dark and dense than the 53rd Open Space area with more conifers—Douglas Firs, hemlocks and cedars. The cedars are the trees with the bark that peels. The hemlock has distinctive "alligator bark" with broad fissures and the Douglas fir has bark that has fissures that are deeper, closer together. The Douglas Fir often has no branches down the its trunk in a mixed forest environment such as this, whereas the hemlock has branches to the bottom, because it's more shade tolerant and can use the lower lighting at the forest floor.

0.8 mi   **Head up this 1/3 mile trail enjoying the natural forest and you'll emerge at the end of SE 54th St at Parkwood Ridge Road. Head up the hill on SE 54th St, crossing 91st Ave SE and 89th Ave SE.**

1.0 mi   **When you reach Island Crest Way, take a right, and then go right again on 53rd Place SE. Soon you'll see another entrance to the 53rd Place SE Open Space Area on your right where we'll duck back onto the trail.** Here you'll have a treetop view of the mixed forest. Also, there is great bird watching in here at the top of the tree canopy!

1.2 mi   As you head down, you'll see evidence of a fire with scorched and burned trees visible from the trail; then you will head into a wetland area at the bottom of the ravine that has lush thickets of water-loving vegetation, and a crazy L-shaped tree.

1.3 mi   **When you get to the split in the path, head down the path to your left which will return you to your starting point in 500 feet.** Next time, try it the other way around— it's an entirely different walk.

1.4 mi   **End at East Mercer Way and SE 53rd Place.**

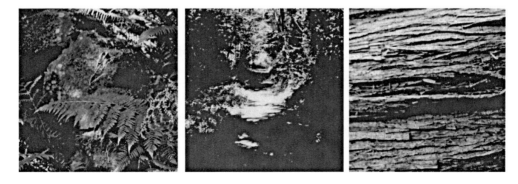

"There is a difference between knowing the path, and walking the path."
Morpheus

Ambitious Walk |

North East Big Loop

This loop starts with the Shoreclub trail, hits the Ellis Pond area and then scoops down and across the North East part of the Island. It takes you through lovely older neighborhoods, shows off some of the Island's great hidden cut-thrus and has some great art and architecture along the way.

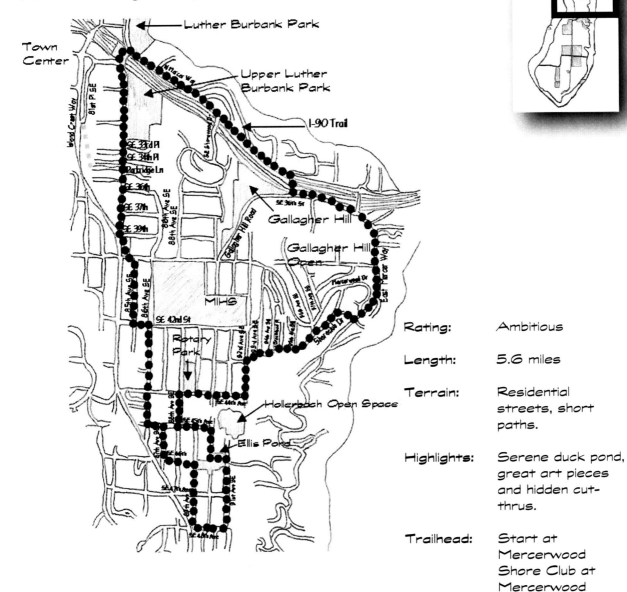

Rating: Ambitious

Length: 5.6 miles

Terrain: Residential streets, short paths.

Highlights: Serene duck pond, great art pieces and hidden cut-thrus.

Trailhead: Start at Mercerwood Shore Club at Mercerwood Drive and East Mercer Way

Guided Tour: North East Big Loop

0.0 mi   **The hike starts on East Mercer Way at the Mercerwood Shore Club.**

Now a wonderful private club, the Mercerwood Shore Club sits on the location of the Ackerson House which in the early 1900s was bought by a Seattle church group for a home for destitute mothers and children. Mothers could board their children there while they worked in Seattle. After a fire, the home closed. In the 1930's a new brick building was built by the Lutheran Church for social services and during WWII it became a home for unwed mothers. During the late 1940's a developer bought the house and remodeled it into a clubhouse with swimming pool and tennis courts for the Mercerwood Shore Club housing development. The current Mercerwood Shore Club was founded in 1953.

Across the street from the Club you'll see a trail sign. Take the path up the hill.

This tree covered path is really fun. Along the way you'll see a fabulous tree house some lucky kids own and a great garden with unique plantings including artichokes, foxgloves and calla lilies.

0.1 mi   **At the top of the trail, take a left and then another left in front of house #4242.**

0.3 mi   **When you come to the top of Shoreclub Drive, take a left. Then another left up the path at the junction of Shoreclub Drive and 95th.**

0.4 mi   **You'll emerge on a cul-de-sac. Go straight to reach 94th and take a left.** Then go right on 43rd and at the end of the block continue straight on the trail.

0.5 mi   **On 92nd take a left then curve right onto 44th.** I often used to walk this route when my son was small. In those days, a couple lived in house #9025 with an amazing cutting garden. In the fall, they would hang scissors on the tree in front of their house with a sign inviting passerby's to cut a

Turn-by-Turn Directions:

- **Start:** Mercerwood Shore Club
- Up Shore Club Trail
- Up Shore Club Drive
- Cut-Thru to SE 43rd St
- Cut Thru to 92nd SE and left
- Right on SE 44th St
- Left on 88th Ave SE
- Left on SE 45th St
- Right on 90th Ave SE to Ellis Pond
- Left on raised trail
- Right on 91st
- Right on 48th Street
- Curve right to cut through
- Cross 47th continuing on 89th
- Left on trail
- Right on 87th Ave SE
- Left on SE 45th St
- Right on 86th Ave SE
- Left at SE 42nd St Cut-thru
- Right on 85th Ave SE
- Cross 40th to Trail through Clise Park
- Left on 39th then right on 84th Ave SE
- At bottom of hill, right into Park-like overpass
- Down ramp, right on I-90 Trail
- Right on North Mercer
- Left on SE 36th
- Right on East Mercer Way
- **End:** Mercerwood Shore Club

bouquet from the garden. I don't walk this way as often as before and haven't seen the sign for many years, but I always think of the owner when I go by—what a lovely thing to do.

0.8 mi   **Soon you'll come to Rotary Park.** Rotary Park began in 1970 as a Rotary Club project and has since evolved into a neighborhood park. It's the highest elevation on the Island and is home to the City's water storage facility. Trails loop the towers and lead into the neighborhoods behind the park.

Take a left on 88th Ave SE past the Library.

The Mercer Island Library is located at the site of the second school on Mercer Island, Allview Heights School, which was built in 1890 on land donated by Vitus Schmid. The Schmid family—some of the Island's first residents—pioneered the Maple Lane area (which we are in now.) Lack of roads made travel to the Little White Schoolhouse in East Seattle impossible for some families, so a local school house was built. The school was closed in 1895 for lack of students and torn down in 1938 with the lumber being used to build the gymnasium at East Seattle School. In the 1950's the land was transferred by the School Board to the Library Board and the Library was opened here in 1955.

Before you go, don't forget to take in the great sculpture in front of the Library, which Islander's love. Titled "Between Two Worlds" this bronze sculpture depicts a boy lying against an impossibly huge rabbit, reading a book with an identical, but life size rabbit nearby. The artist, Georgia Gerber, wanted the piece to encourage involvement—inviting children to climb on the piece and read along with the boy. Many times I've picked up my daughter to find her reading her new library books atop the rabbit's back or sitting right next to the boy. The piece certainly speaks to the "ability of the written word to free the imagination"

1.0 mi   **Take left on SE 45th Street.** At the corner of 90th Ave SE, you can peek into the Hollerbach Open Space area—at 5.18 acres, it's one of several unimproved open space areas owned by the City.

1.1 mi   **Go right on 90th Ave SE.** This quiet street has some wonderful old foliage from by-gone days. People in this neighborhood seem to enjoy their yards. There are some enviable vegetable gardens along here, and a great yard with some wonderful old fruit trees—including apple and cherries—and a huge plum tree.

1.2 mi   **The road ends at Ellis Pond.** Ellis Pond is a natural pond tucked between homes on the top of the Island. Many bird and animal species can be found in this lovely four-acre pond habitat. Ellis Pond is a product of the care provided by the community that surrounds it. Local neighbors have planted native trees and shrubs and been great stewards for the park.

When you are done hanging out with the ducks, take a left across the raised walkway, enjoying the fruits of the neighborhood native plant restoration efforts. Then take a right on 91st Avenue.

1.4 mi   At 47th Street, you'll see some pillars on your left. This marks the top of the 47th Street Open Space, a 1½ acre area that runs between here and East Mercer Way—another one of those unimproved city-owned areas. As it stands, there are no official cut-thrus between East Mercer and the middle of the island from the Shore Club to 53rd SE. Wouldn't this be a perfect one?

The home at #4744 must be home to an artist—there's always something fun to see in this yard—a cool log mailbox post made into a dog, a wire body form, an alien on a pillar...you never know what you'll find here!

1.5 mi	Take a right on 48ᵗʰ Street, crossing 90ᵗʰ. At the curve in the road, you'll see a cut-thru to Island Crest Way—we'll continue curving right, staying on the road. At the end of the road, take the path that cuts-thru to 47ᵗʰ Street.
1.7 mi	Cross 47ᵗʰ, heading straight on 89ᵗʰ.
1.9 mi	You'll see two trails on your right that head back to Ellis Pond. Across from the second one, take a left on the path, going away from the Pond. Continue straight across 88ᵗʰ, continuing on 46ᵗʰ Street. If you take a left at 87ᵗʰ, you'll find another cut-thru to Island Crest Way, but we'll take a right today.
2.2 mi	At SE 45ᵗʰ, take a left and then a right on 86ᵗʰ Avenue SE—skirting the property of Emmanuel Episcopal Church—complete with garden and old fruit trees. A cherry orchard known as Melhorn Orchard was located on this block-square tract of land originally homesteaded by the Schmid family. Emmanuel Church purchased the property when it sought parish status in 1955 after a long history on the island. Emmanuel was the first church on Mercer Island. The church was started as a mission in 1909 and the small congregation met in a home in East Seattle. In 1914, the church was able to raise funds to build a small, rustic church on what is now West Mercer Way and SE 27ᵗʰ and later a Guild Hall was added east of the Church almost next to the Boys and Girls Club. Soon the Church and Guild had become a key aspect of the social fabric of East Seattle—prompting an old timer to explain that "everyone was an Episcopalian in those days." The Emmanuel Episcopal Church on Mercer Island is still going strong after more than 100 years here in its relatively new location.
2.3 mi	You'll see Maple Lane on your left, but continue straight.
	The Maple Lane area was homesteaded in the late 1800's by Vitus Schmid, a wagon-maker's apprentice from Baden, Germany. He and John Wensler, a cobbler from Chicago, filed a 160 acre claim on this part of the Island and built a cabin here in 1876. Schmid and Wensler left after a tree fell on their hand-built cabin, but Schmid returned with a wife and family in 1978—filing a new claim. His cabin was here—in the area now known as Maple Lane—until 1954 when it was torn down to make way for modern houses.
2.5 mi	At the stop sign at 42ⁿᵈ Street, take a left on the trail, then go right on 85ᵗʰ.
2.9 mi	Cross 40ᵗʰ and take a left. Then go right on the trail that goes through Clise Park. Clise Park was named after Charles Clise, a Seattle businessman. Clise bought the Fortuna Park property after World War II, built the "Lower Shorewood Apartment Complex" in the 1950's (which is now part of the Covenant Shores community), and ran it for 25 years.
3.0 mi	The trail comes out on SE 39ᵗʰ—take a left on 39ᵗʰ and then a right on 84ᵗʰ Ave SE. The Mercer Island Presbyterian Church is quite a significant building as it was designed by the famous architect Paul Thiry in 1962. Paul Thiry is known nationally as the "father of Northwest modernism"—having brought a regional variant of European Modernism to the Northwest in the mid-1930's. The church is an example of Thiry's interest in experimentation with concrete building technology and has clear windows that transparently brings the world into the church.
3.3 mi	Coninute down 84ᵗʰ. And soon you'll see Upper Luther Burbank Park on your right. Upper Luther Burbank Park is an unimproved part of Luther Burbank Park below. There are some

informal and short trails in here, but mostly it's used by the kids in the neighborhood for mountain biking. As of late, the neighborhood has been involved in restoration project on the parcel as well.

84th Avenue is called "snake hill" because it snakes down the hill toward town. This is a great alternative walking route to all things on the North End of the Island—much nicer than Island Crest Way. Most of the roads here dead end, but 35th does have a pathway (cut-thru) that gets you to the middle part of town. You'll see Town Center on your left at the bottom of the hill.

3.7 mi **Take a right on 82nd Avenue and then a right on the path, staying right at the junction.** This beautiful little overpass is one of the most little known and underutilized parts of the Island. This park is part of the Lid Park project—which capped the i-90 bridge. It's a one-of-a-kind park built on top of a concrete lid covering a half-mile stretch of I-90 and was completed in 1994. The lid was intended to muffle the noise and reconnect neighborhoods that were severed when the old Sunset Highway became I-90. The Park is highly unique. Funding for the project was approved in the 1976 environmental-impact statement and was locked in by a federal court decision, thus protecting it against the government frugality of the 1980's.

The sculpture of the eagle on your left is called 'Mercy'. The piece was created by Sara Malljohani who said this about the piece: "The bald eagle is America's symbol of pride and glory, sacred to the Native People and later adopted by the new Americans. Our compassion, our mercy has brought it back from the edge of extinction to which we drove it. Can we also commit our energy to the recovery of the wild Northwest and salmon who we have driven to the same precipice? We are all related."

3.9 mi **Take in the big view at the top of the ramp, then head down to meet up with the I-90 Trail that parallels I-90. At the bottom of the ramp take a right.** This section of trail is a part of the Mountains to Sound Greenway which is a regional trail system that is very close to offering a continuous trail from Seattle, across the Cascades to eastern Washington. This path is well used by bike commuters on weekdays and recreational riders on weekends. Keep to the right and keep an eye out for fast bikes along here!

4.4 mi **Cross Shorewood Drive and continue on the path.**

4.6 mi **The path drops down and soon you will see Covenant Shores Retirement Community on your left.** In the early 1900's this location was hopping. Fortuna Park was the destination of excursion boats that came from Seattle for a daylong outing. The Park was created by Captain John Anderson, who ran the ferry and included playfields, a dance hall, swimming beach, rental boats, food and beverage booths. After Anderson's death, the property was sold to a hop farmer from Eastern Washington who planned a Bavarian village on the property, but the plan stopped when he died. The next owner was Charles Clise (remember Clise Park?) who built apartments on the property (Lower Shorewood). The complex traded hands a few times before being bought by Covenant Retirements Communities and making it into Covenant Shores today. In fact, the dining hall that the residents use today was the Dance Hall for Fortuna Park. Ironically, some of those dancing to dinner now were also dancing in that hall in years past. My friend Lucy Phillips, who is a resident there today, remembers going there on the ferry as a child with her father for the French/Italian picnics that were held there.

4.8 mi **At the stop sign, take a right on North Mercer Way.** On the corner of North Mercer Way and SE 36th (Gallagher Hill) there is a great sculpture of a flock of birds, appropriately called Flock.

4.9 mi **Cross the street and take a left on SE 36th where you will pass the city buildings on your left.** The "9611" building and the 14 acres of land surrounding it were traded with

Farmer's New World Life Insurance Company for the land downtown where their headquarters are located today. City Hall, the Police Station and the City Maintenance facilities were built here after a political battle and public vote between locating the city buildings here or on the Mercerdale Park property downtown. Don't miss the great stainless steel sculpture at the front entrance. Called "Mercer Island Sentinel;" it was created by Valdis Zarin in 1990.

5.1 mi   **At the corner of SE 36th and East Mercer Way, take a right.** In front of you is the East Channel Bridge that gave Mercer Islanders the first non-boat access to the Island. The first bridge to Mercer Island was opened in November 1923. The East Channel Bridge connected this area known as Barnabie Point on northeast Mercer Island to Enatai in Bellevue. The wooden bridge served the island until 1939 when the next bridge was built—and just in time. In the last few years of its life, it became so rickety that the school bus made the children get out and walk across the bridge. The opening of the Bridge made the North End into a thoroughfare, changing the traffic patterns and eventually driving the move of the commercial center of Mercer Island from East Seattle to the central district. Seattle drivers would get on a ferry from Leschi, cross the lake, drive off on Mercer Island at Roanoke Dock and across the north end of the Island, and cross the bridge to the eastside.

You'll pass the boat launch and Herzl-Ner-Tamid Synagogue on your left, and the Jewish Community Center and French American School on your right.

5.4 mi   **Soon you'll pass 40th on your right. Continue on East Mercer Way.**

In 1912, this corner was the location of Barnabie School which served the children living on the northeast side of the Island with one room and one teacher. If you head up 40th a bit, you'll see neighborhoods that still carry the Barnabie name. If you take a right up 40th, there is a great cut-thru to the top of the Island—offering a good way to the pool and Youth Theater.

5.6 mi   **You'll have some nice views along the way and then will find yourself back at your starting point at the Mercerwood Shore Club.**

"An early morning walk is a blessing for the whole day."
Henry David Thoreau

45

Family Walk |
Island Crest Neighborhood Loop

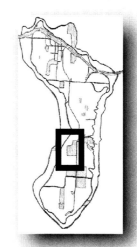

This fun-filled loop will keep young children moving, active and engaged. Be sure to bring a picnic or snack as there are tables in the children's playground (where the hike ends), and even a covered area for unexpected bad weather. Bathrooms are easily accessible. This walk should be experienced in every season. In summer it's cool under the tree canopy; in spring the beautiful trilliums provide a treasure hunt of sorts for the kids; in the fall the leaves are ablaze with color and soft underfoot; and a snowstorm provides a welcome quiet that doesn't seem possible so close to home.

Rating: Family Hike

Length: 1.5 miles

Terrain: Some hills, quiet and forested, some residential streets.

Highlights: Quiet hiking trails, a suspension bridge, a forested children's playground, and horses.

Trailhead: Start at Island Crest Park, off Island Crest Way, just south of SE 54th St. Bathrooms, picnic tables and a covered shelter are available in Deane's Children's Park.

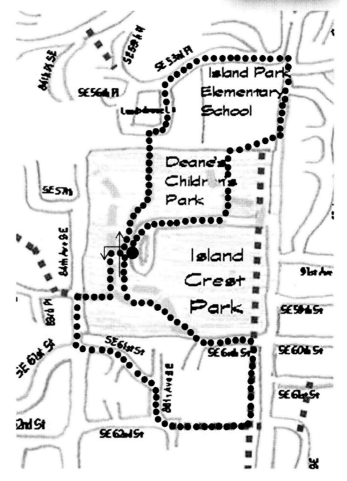

Guided Walk: Island Crest Neighborhood Loop

0.0 mi The hike starts in the main parking lot of Island Crest Park—the one located near the ball fields. Use the restrooms at the ballpark if you need to before heading out. On the northwest side of the parking lot you will see a trail marker sign pointing into the woods. Follow the trail down the hill.

0.1 mi At the bottom of the hill, you will find a wooden suspension bridge. Head across, but be careful! It can be a bit wobbly and slippery! At the far end of the bridge, take the trail to your left. Continue along the path, staying right at the first trail junction, and going straight at the second.

40-acre Island Crest Park is a wonderful reminder of the way the Island was not long ago--wooded and wild.

0.4 mi In a quarter mile or so, you will come to a set of stairs that lead out of the woods (don't worry, you'll be back!) If you headed straight down SE 59ᵗʰ, you would see a path on the right that will take you down a ravine to Groveland Beach Park—but for this walk, we'll take a left on 84ᵗʰ Ave SE and go a long block. Just past the end of the Park, take a left at SE 61ˢᵗ St.

0.5 mi At 86ᵗʰ Ave SE. take a right and then a left on SE 62ⁿᵈ St. The street will end and turn into a little lane next to Stevenson's Stables. Meander down the path, enjoying the horses.

The five acre Stevenson Farm is one of two places on the Island where horses are stabled, the other being the Saddle Club near Sunnybeam School. Horses were once a critical part of island life. The south end of the Island especially, remained quite rural with poor roads until the building boom of the 60's and 70's. Many Island residents made their way to school or the north part of the Island by horseback.

0.7 mi When you reach Island Crest Ave, take a left and continue about a block until you reach SE 60ᵗʰ Street, then turn left, heading west until you reach a cut-thru at the southwest corner of the ball fields. The path will be on your right and begins in front of the house numbered 8631.

0.8 mi Re-enter Island Crest Park and walk north back toward the parking lot, skirting the ball field to the left. Behind the batting cages, you will see a second entrance to the wooded paths west of the park. Take a left and head down

Turn-by-Turn Directions:

- **Start:** Island Crest Park, off ICW just south of SE 54ᵗʰ St
- Down trail off parking lot
- Cross suspension bridge, then left on trail
- Right at first trail junction
- Straight at the second
- Left on 84ᵗʰ Ave SE
- Left on SE 61ˢᵗ St
- Right on 86ᵗʰ Ave SE
- Left on SE 62ⁿᵈ St
- Left on Island Crest Way
- Left on SE 60ᵗʰ St
- Right on trail into the park
- Left on path into the woods
- Right at first junction
- Straight at suspension bridge
- Right on Landsdowne Lane
- Right on 53ʳᵈ Pl
- Right on Island Crest
- Right Into Deane's Children's Park
- **End:** Island Crest Park

the stairs, back into the woods. Follow the path, turning right at the first junction and crossing a little wooden platform.

0.9 mi   The forested path will return you to the suspension bridge, but this time don't cross it or turn up the hill toward your starting point, but instead head straight at the junction (north). Eventually the trail ends at Landsdowne Lane. Take a right on Landsdowne and then another right on SE 53rd Place and head up the hill. At the top of 53rd, you can almost see the 53rd SE Open Space over the top of the hill. The open space has great trails for another day.

1.1 mi   At Island Crest take a right, or if school isn't in session, cut across the school yard.

1.3 mi   At the south end of the school yard, just beyond the covered play area there is a little gate that will take you into Deane's Children's Park where our hike ends. If school is in session, you can continue to travel on Island Crest back to the Park entrance and Deane's Park will be on your right.

Explore the trails and playground, eat lunch at a picnic table and use the restrooms. Don't miss the dragon hidden in the woods! Deane's Park is named after Lola and Phil Deane, long time Mercer Island residents, for their community service and support for developing the Park. Lola Deane was a registered nurse and entrepreneur, who started our very own Island Books in 1973. Phil Deane was a pediatrician on the island, establishing Mercer Island Pediatrics in the 1970's. Phil died in 2007, but Lola is still active with park initiatives on another island—San Juan Island.

1.5 mi   When you're finished in the park, your starting point is just a minute away. From the south end of the park, you should be able to see the Island Crest Park ball fields where this walk began.

48

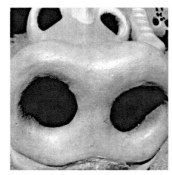  

"Golf is a good walk spoiled."
Mark Twain

49

Moderate Walk |

West Side Park and Beach Loop

This 1.6 mile loop has a steep descent and climb, but is worth the fun of going from woods to waterfront and back again. The hike stretches between two great parks—Island Crest and Groveland Beach, so plan in some time to relax and enjoy them.

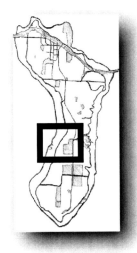

Rating:	Moderate
Length:	1.6 miles
Terrain:	Steep forested trails and residential streets.
Highlights:	Quiet hiking trails, suspension bridge, beach, dock.
Trailhead:	Start at Island Crest Park, Off Island Crest Way, just south of SE 54th St. Bathrooms and picnic tables are available at the ball field and at Groveland Park.

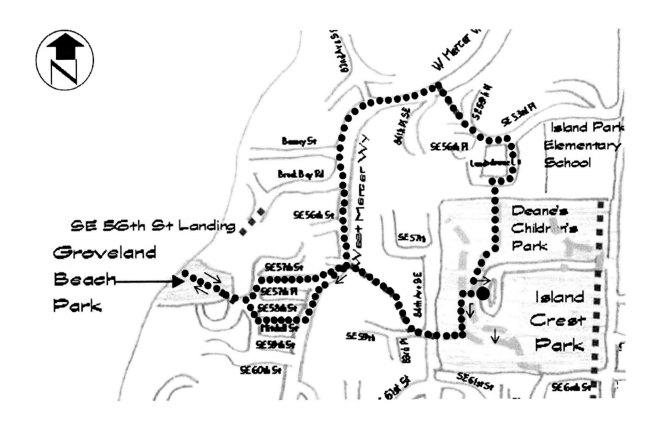

Guided Tour: West Side Park & Beach Loop

0.0 mi Head to Island Crest Park, using the restrooms at the ballpark if you need to before heading out. The walk starts from the main parking lot near the ball fields. On the northwest side of the parking lot you will see a trail marker sign pointing into the woods. Follow the trail down the hill.

0.1 mi At the bottom of the hill, you will find the suspension bridge. Head across, but be careful! It can be a bit wobbly and slippery! Once on the other side, take a left and continue along the path. Take a right at the first trail junction, then continue straight at the second.

Island Crest Park gives us a feel for what Mercer Island used to look like. The Island was essentially a forest in the middle of the lake. The trees you see here, however, are a second growth of trees. Logging on the Island started in the 1880's and it was largely logged off by the turn of the century. The trees around you are probably not more than 100 years old, but the size of stumps in the parks tells the history.

Turn-by-Turn Directions:

- **Start:** Island Crest Park
- **Go** Down the hill off parking lot, across suspension bridge
- Left, right, straight in woods until you reach 84th Ave SE
- Cross street and go straight on 59th St
- Right on path into woods
- Left on West Mercer Way
- Right on SE 57th St to Groveland Beach Park
- Back up SE 58th St
- Left on West Mercer
- Right on trail just past 84th Pl SE
- Right on SE 53rd Pl
- Right on Landowne Lane
- Path into woods
- Left at suspension bridge
- **End:** Island Crest Park

0. 2 mi Eventually, you will come to a set of stairs that lead out of the woods on the corner of 84th Ave SE and SE 59th St. Cross 84th and head down SE 59th—soon on your right you will see an unmarked set of stairs down the ravine. Head down into this beautiful wooded area being careful on the wooden bridges when they are wet, as they can be slippery!

0.4 mi The trail emerges at a house (#5710). Continue down the paved road to the right of the house until you reach West Mercer Way. Looking to the left from this corner, you can see the trail sign that points toward Groveland Park. Take a left on West Mercer, crossing when safe, then turn right on 57th St and head down to the Park.

0.5 mi Spend a little time enjoying Groveland Park. You will need to travel down a steep paved walkway, but it's worth the trek. Here you will find beautiful views, picnic tables, a playground, a beach, a volleyball court, bathrooms and even a dock for fishing. In the early 1900's this area was originally a bible camp, offering a gathering place for off island religious groups. The property was bought by the city in 1965 for a beach park.

0.8 mi When you're ready to return, head back up to the Groveland Park parking lot and proceed up SE 58th St, taking a left on West Mercer Way. At this point, you can return the way you came, or add some distance by walking 3/10 of a mile north on West Mercer Way to the cut-thru at Lansdowne Lane. To reach Lansdowne Lane, take a left on West Mercer Way which curves its way north. Stay on the left side of the road to face traffic on this curvy road.

0.9 mi   The trail sign you see along the way on the left at SE 56th St used to lead to the water access point at SE 56th St Landing, but it no longer goes through. To get to the 56th Street Landing, use Brook Bay Road instead, just north of the sign. Water access is found between house #10 and #8. The hill is steep and the landing generally isn't worth the walk unless you want a little more exercise.

1.2 mi   Continue on West Mercer way, curving around about 3/10 of a mile until you see 84th Place SE. Just past 84th Place SE you will see three white pillars in front of a cut-thru on the right. Carefully cross the street and proceed up the hill, skirting the house at #8395 ending on SE 53rd Place. Looking up the hill, you will see a trail marker above you.

1.4 mi   Walk up the hill and take a right at the trail sign on Lansdowne Lane and curve up the hill until you see a second trail marker on the left. Return to Island Crest Park by walking on the path to right of house #5345.

1.6 mi   Head through the woods. You will be on a trail below Island Park Elementary School, eventually ending up back at the suspension bridge. Take a left up the hill to return to the parking lot where we started.

"To lead people, walk behind them."
Lao Tzu

Moderate Walk |
East Side Forest Loop

This loop connects trails in Pioneer Park, Parkwood Ridge Open Space, and Island Crest Park for an interesting 3.2 mile hike. These three parks provide some of the quietest forest hiking on the Island, while being only minutes from civilization. Directions for this hike start at the South End shopping center taking a counter-clockwise route, but the hike offers just as much fun the other direction or starting from different points along the way. There is some hiking on East Mercer Way that can be busy during commute times, and a crossing of busy Island Crest Way, so plan your hike times accordingly.

Rating: Ambitious

Length: 3.2 miles

Terrain: Forested trails, some residential streets. Two major elevation changes (ascent and decent) with the rest relatively flat.

Highlights: Lots of time in the quiet woods, trilliums in the spring.

Trailhead: Start at the South End shopping center at SE 68th St and 84th Ave SE.

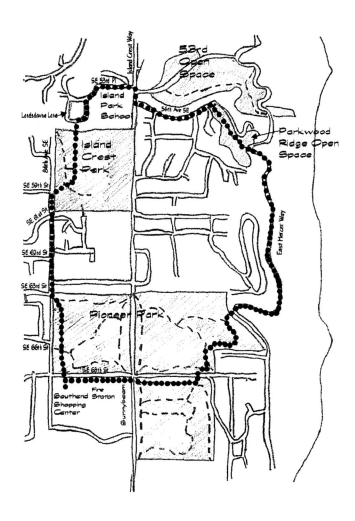

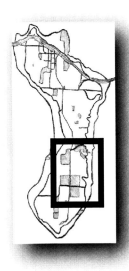

Guided Tour: East Side Forest Loop

0.0 mi   **Start at the South End shopping center. Go right (east) on 68ᵗʰ Ave SE.**

The South End shopping center is a much needed resource for South End residents—bringing coffee, groceries, gas and restaurants closer to home for many Island residents. The center was opened in 1961, when the South End was still quite rural, amid a zoning and landscaping controversy. It was, in fact, the last rezoning and development plan done under county jurisdiction. After that the planning and design was managed by the Islands' Town and City Governments.

0.1 mi   **You'll see the Fire Station on your right (opened in 1961), and on your left is a great piece of art.**

This piece called "Mythical Bird" was created by an award-winning sculptor named Dudley Carter from Redmond Washington. Dudley Carter was born in Canada and worked in logging until the depression when he turned to art. His art is known internationally, and much of his work was in the form of totem poles (one of which can be found at the entrance to Marymoor Park). He used an axe to create his large works and continued creating new works until he died at the age of 100 in 1992. Do you see the raven, coyote, birds and female forms in this sculpture?

0.2 mi   **Continue along SE 68ᵗʰ Street, to Lakeview School.**

This historic building was built in 1918 when the local school district voted to build a schoolhouse by issuing local improvement bonds. All elementary grades were taught at the school and then students were ferried to Seattle or Bellevue for high school until 1941, when the roads had been improved enough to bus students to East Seattle School. The small cottage on the property was built at the same time as the school to house the teacher. Today, it is the home of the Pioneer Park Youth Club's caretakers.

Turn-by-Turn Directions:

- **Start:** South End Shopping Center
- Right on 68ᵗʰ Street
- Cross Island Crest Way
- Continue straight on Pioneer Park Trail
- Cross 68ᵗʰ Street at crosswalk
- Right on trail
- Left into park
- Right at first junction
- Right at second junction down ravine
- At split in the trail take a right
- Left on East Mercer Way
- Left on Parkwood Ridge Open Space trail
- Straight on Parkwood Ridge
- Continue on SE 54ᵗʰ Street
- Cross Island Crest Way
- East on SE 53ʳᵈ, down hill
- Left on Landsdown Lane
- Left on trail into Island Crest Park
- Straight at suspension bridge
- Right at trail junction
- Left on 84ᵗʰ Ave SE
- Left into Pioneer Park, then right on trail
- **End:** South End Shopping Center

Today, the property is owned and managed by a small volunteer group, The Pioneer Youth Club, which started out as the "South End Improvement Club" a citizens group that was extremely active until the 1970's bringing services such as roads, water and power to South End residents. In 1974, the group traded the 10 acre parcel of land they owned (that now houses IMS, Lakeridge and the South Mercer Playfields) for this smaller tract that the school district owned—allowing new schools to be built on the South End of Mercer Island.

The 4.35 acre property is now home to Sunnybeam School, Mercer Island Saddle Club, and the Children's Dance Conservatory. Sunnybeam School was started in 1957 by Nuky Fellows and Eleanor Wolf. Nuky had grown up on the island, a member of the pioneer Vinal family that arrived on the island in 1908. In 1981, Eleanor Wolf died and Nuky Fellows retired in 1984, so a parent volunteer board was formed to run the school. The school still houses a pre-school to Island youth after over 60 years!

Another long-time resident of the property is The Children's Dance Conservatory, directed by Susan Valencia, for over 25 years. This Royal Academy of Dance (RAD) school puts on a lovely youth Nutcracker performance every year which should not be missed. The Mercer Island Saddle Club reminds us of the wonderful rural past of Mercer Island. Horses are stabled and trained on the grounds and riders utilize the nearby trails of Pioneer Park for enjoyment.

0.3 mi   **When you get to Island Crest, cross the street, entering Pioneer Park, and continuing east on the path that skirts 68th Street.**

At 120 acres, Pioneer Park is the largest natural space on Mercer Island. Its three-40 acre natural woodland parcels give visitors a feel for what the Island must have looked like in the mid-1800's. Although the entire Island had been logged clean of its virgin timber by the turn of the century, the property is an amazing example of how our ecosystem naturally restores itself when left all alone. Many of the trees in the park are over 100 feet tall and 100 years old, while stumps from the original logging effort can still be found today.

The Park property was privately owned until 1931 when it was willed to the University of Washington by Mrs. Maud Walker-Ames, whose family ironically was one of the most prominent and wealthy logging families in the Northwest. Interestingly, she also willed their family home to the UW, and the 40-room, 12,788 square foot, brick mansion—colloquially referred to as 808—is still home to the University President and his family, and acts as a bustling social venue for University events.

When Mercer Island was incorporated in 1960, the city started planning for a park system and learned that the "university properties" (as they were known) were available. The city passed a bond in 1964 to purchase the land to allow islanders to get out into nature. In 1969, it seemed imminent that 80 acres of the park would be cleared for a municipal golf course and the prospect came forth again in the 1980's with both efforts defeated.

The Park today contains 6.6 miles of trails for walking and limited trails for horseback riding, which have been kept in a natural state. An old, but still relevant detailed resource about the park is called "Pioneer Park—A Natural History" that can be found online (see Resources). It would be wonderful if the Mercer Island Parks and Recreation group did another revision to this guide as it really helps bring the Park alive.

0.4 mi   **Cross the street at the cross walk, and take a right on the trail. At the end of the Park, take a left deeper into the trees, then right and right again at the two junctions. You'll descend into the ravine.** This trail that takes you from Pioneer Park to East Mercer Way is in a parcel officially named Engstrom Open Space. In 2006, longtime islanders Ken and Margaret Quarles transferred 7 acres of their property to the city earning honors as Mercer Island Citizen's of the Year as well as a fond place in the hearts of Mercer Island walkers. The property is named the Engstrom Open Space, in honor of Margaret's father Oscar who originally purchased the land in 1925 as a summer get-away. Oscar Engstrom built their year-round home here in 1955, and the Quarles have lived in the original waterfront home since 1961.

0.7 mi   **At the bottom of the ravine, take a right, cross the bridge and then another right and you will exit the park at East Mercer Way. Take a left on East Mercer Way. You will be gently curving north. Be sure to walk against traffic on this stretch and keep an eye out for bicycles.**

1.5 mi   7/10th of a mile down the road you will see the entrance to the Parkwood Ridge Open Space area. Take a left up the trail. Be sure to stay on the trail as you're crossing private property here. Parkwood Ridge Open Space is a 3.8 naturally wooded parcel that connects East Mercer Way with the Parkwood neighborhood above. This new trail was opened in 2007, with a local Boy Scout achieving his Eagle Scout Award by coordinating with the Parks Natural Resources Coordinator on slope stabilization and re-vegetation efforts along several sections of the new trail. Over 100 native trees were installed throughout the Open Space during the project.

1.8 mi   **You will exit the trail at Parkwood Ridge Way. Take a left up the hill and then continue straight on SE 54th St. At Island Crest Way, carefully cross the street, go to the right of the school parking lot and head west down SE 53rd Place.** Island Park Elementary is one of the three elementary schools on the island. It was opened in 1957 to meet the needs of the building boom on the island in the 50's and 60's.

2.2 mi   **At Landowne Lane you will see a trail sign. Take a left, and then another left at the at the second trail sign to enter Island Crest Park. The path is to the right of the house #5341.** The trail will take you through towering trees and lush ferns. 40-acre Island Crest Park is another one of the island's wooded and wild areas. It also includes the ballpark, tennis courts and Deane's Children's Park, closer to Island Crest Way.

2.4 mi   **At the suspension bridge you will come to a junction. The trail to your left will lead to the Island Crest Park parking lot, the right will lead across the suspension bridge. Continue straight here.**

2.6 mi   **At the trail junction, stay right. The left hand fork will take you up to the Island Crest Ball Fields. Eventually, the trail will wind through and emerge at 84th Ave SE. Take a left and walk along the street until you reach the northwest corner of Pioneer Park at SE 64th. Take a left into the Park, then staying right to run parallel to 84th.**

3.2 mi   **You will emerge at the South End Shopping Center.**

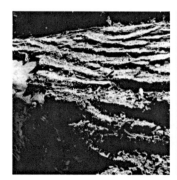 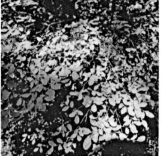 

"A line is a dot that went for a walk."
Paul Klee

Family Walk |
Pioneer Park Forest Fun

A Mercer Island 'classic.' You'll almost forget you're in the suburbs during this wonderful forested trek that hits all three sections of the South End's Pioneer Park. It's full of fun ascents and descents through the natural terrain of Mercer Island; fascinating information about our logging past and the forests natural rejuvenation; safe street crossings, and even a place to stop for a hot chocolate or lemonade at the conclusion. Throw a carrot in your pocket to feed the horses at the Saddle Club if you're inclined.

Rating:	Family
Length:	1.6 miles
Terrain:	Forested paths, mostly flat with one big descent and ascent.
Highlights:	Quiet, natural forest plus horses.
Trailhead:	Start at the South End shopping center on SE 68th Street

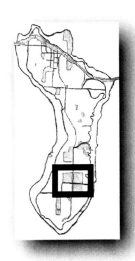

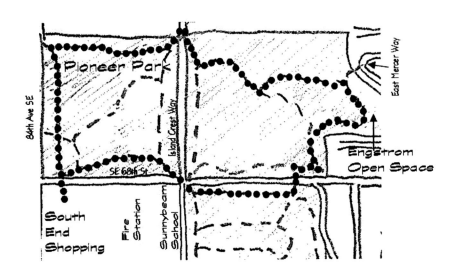

Guided Tour: Pioneer Park Forest Fun

0.0 mi   Starting at the southwest corner of the South End Shopping Center, cross 68th Street heading into Pioneer Park near the picnic table. Take a left on the perimeter trail, then a right, staying on the perimeter of the Park.

At 120 acres, Pioneer Park is the largest natural space on Mercer Island. Its three-40 acre natural woodland parcels give visitors a feel for what the island must have looked like in the mid-1800's. Although the entire Island had been logged clean of its virgin timber by the turn of the century, the property is an amazing example of how our ecosystem naturally restores itself when left all alone. Many of the trees in the park are over 100 feet tall and 100 years old, while the stumps from the original logging effort can still be found today.

The park property was privately owned until 1931 when it was willed to the University of Washington by Mrs. Maud Walker-Ames, whose family ironically was one of the most prominent and wealthy logging families in the Northwest. Interestingly, she also willed their family home to the UW, and the 40-room, 12,788 square foot, brick mansion—colloquially referred to as 808—is still home to the University President and his family, and acts as a bustling social venue for University events.

Turn-by-Turn Directions:

- **Start:** South End Shopping Center
- Cross 68th Street and enter Pioneer Park near the picnic table.
- Take a left on the trail that skirts the park—then a right, staying on the perimeter trail.
- Continue straight at the first two junctions, then right, continuing on the perimeter trail.
- Go left out of the park onto Island Crest Way
- Cross the street at the crosswalk.
- Go right on Island Crest Way, reentering the park.
- Take a left on the dirt path
- Take another left heading down into the ravine.
- At the bottom of the ravine, veer right, heading back up the trail.
- At the rise, take a left and then another left.
- Go right when you reach the trail that parallels SE 68th Street
- Cross the street (left) at the cross walk
- Take a right on the trail
- Cross Island Crest Way
- **End:** South End Shopping Center

When Mercer Island was incorporated in 1960, the city started planning for a park system and learned that the "university properties" (as they were known) were available. The city passed a bond in 1964 to purchase the land to allow Islanders to get out into nature. In 1969, it seemed imminent that 80 acres of the Park would be cleared for a municipal golf course and the prospect came forth again in the 1980's with both efforts defeated.

The Park today contains 6.6 miles of trails for walking and limited trails for horseback riding, which have been kept in a natural state. An old, but still relevant detailed resource about the park is called "Pioneer Park—A Natural History" that can be found online on the MI city web site. It would be wonderful if the Mercer Island Parks and Recreation group did another revision to this guide as it really helps bring the Park alive.

0.2 mi Continue straight past the forest information sign, and two trails that head to the interior of the Park. At the far end of the Park, take a right, continuing on the perimeter trail.

The informational signs that you see were created as an Eagle Scout project of Alan Cordova in 2000. The Scouts do many projects on the Island—favorites often having to do with the parks and paths.

0.6 mi When you get near Island Crest Way, you'll see a well-used horse trail on your right. We'll take a left and head out of the Park, going left on Island Crest Way, crossing 63rd, and then crossing Island Crest Way at the cross walk. Then take a right, heading back into the north east quadrant of the park. The paved path will dip down and soon you will see a dirt trail on your left. Take the dirt trail, called Overlook Trail, left back into the park.

The natural vegetation in the park is a prime example of the forests of lowland western Washington—it is typical of the Western Hemlock Zone of the Northwest Pacific slope. In the Park you will see many towering Western Hemlocks, as well as Douglas Firs, Western Red Cedars. You'll also see Big-Leaf Maples, Madronnas and Red Alders in abundance. The forest is also filled with elderberry, huckleberries, Oregon Grape, salal, multiple types of ferns, devils club, youth-on-age, and foam flowers. My favorites—the trilliums—come out in abundance here in the spring, making this a must-do walk when they are blooming. The reason that this type of forest is called a Western Hemlock forest, even though there are many other types of trees and plants, is that if you let the forest grow naturally, over time it would end up as mostly Western Hemlock.

However, this forest is not progressing as is expected. Pioneer Park is victim to a naturally occurring disease called Phellinus Weirii that causes root rot and is taking a considerable toll on the Douglas Firs in the forest. The condition is spread through root-to-root contact, so affected trees are found in large pockets throughout the forest. You can see one here—the clearing in the forest as you first enter. Since the disease is naturally occurring and many of the strategies for stopping its progression require significant tree removal, the city has taken the approach of letting it occur naturally.

0.8 mi At the first trail junction, take a left down the Ravine Trail.

Just as you drop down into the ravine, look down the ravine on your left and you'll see a very, very large stump. This is one of the many artifacts of the logging days in the late 1800's. As mentioned, this whole Island was clear cut and what you are seeing is primarily second growth. If you look carefully at the large stump, you can see holes in the sides of the stump. These holes held the "springboards" that the loggers inserted and stood on so that they could get higher up to a narrow part of the tree so they could saw it down faster by hand. Kind of a cool example of a logging artifact.

Soon, you'll see a great example of a "nurse log"—the amazing way that a new tree grows out of the remnants of a log or stump. This tall stump was a Douglas Fir that was harvested over 100 years ago. The tree growing out of it is a Hemlock.

When you get to the little bridge, stop for a minute and look at the big trees. My friend Wayne Gullstad taught me how to tell the difference between the trees by looking at the bark. The Hemlock has a distinctive Alligator-like skin and often has branches to the bottom. The Cedar has bark that peels and tends to not have branches down the trunk. The Douglas Fir has deeper fissures and also doesn't have branches to the forest floor.

He also had me grab the little evergreen tree growing below the bridge and taught me firsthand how to identify a Spruce Tree (also known as an "ouch" tree—go ahead, try it.) Apparently, Boeing located in the Pacific Northwest because of the spruce—it's a strong and light wood—and was perfect for building the first airplanes. Although, there are not many spruce growing in this forest.

0.9 mi   **At the bottom of the ravine, you'll see a trail that veers left. That trail hits East Mercer Way. We'll continue to our right, up a gentle slope atop the trees.**

The area you are looking down upon is actually adjacent to Pioneer Park. It is the Engstrom Open Space area. In 2006, longtime islanders Ken and Margaret Quarles transferred 7 acres of their property to the city earning honors as Mercer Island Citizen's of the Year as well as a fond place in the hearts of Mercer Island walkers. The section of property is officially named the Engstrom Open Space, in honor of Margaret's father Oscar who originally purchased the land in 1925 as a summer get-away. Oscar Engstrom built their year-round home here in 1955, and the Quarles have lived in the original waterfront home since 1961. This generous donation allowed the creation of this gorgeous ravine trail and a new connection between East Mercer Way and Pioneer Park.

Don't miss the two amazing examples of those "nurse stumps" on the way up.

1.0 mi   **When you reach the top of the ravine, continue on the trail. At the first split, take a left and then another left at the second. When the trail nears the road, take a right. Then go left at the crosswalk to enter the third quadrant of Pioneer Park. Go right on the path, going parallel to 68th Street.**

1.4 mi   **Cross Island Crest Way and you'll come to Sunnybeam School in the historic Lakeview School.**

This historic building was built in 1918 when the local school district voted to build a schoolhouse by issuing local improvement bonds. All elementary grades were taught at the school and students were ferried to Seattle or Bellevue for high school, until 1941, when the roads had been improved enough to bus students to East Seattle School. The small cottage on the property was built at the same time as the school to house the teacher. Today, it is the home of the Pioneer Park Youth Club's caretakers.

Today, the property is owned and managed by a small volunteer group, The Pioneer Youth Club, which started out as the "South End Improvement Club" a citizens group that was extremely active until the 1970's bringing services such as roads, water and power to South End residents. In 1974, the group traded the 10 acre parcel of land they owned (that now houses IMS, Lakeridge and the South Mercer Playfields) for this smaller tract that the school district owned—allowing new schools to be built on the South End of Mercer Island.

The 4.35 acre property is now home to Sunnybeam School, Mercer Island Saddle Club, and the Children's Dance Conservatory. Sunnybeam School was started in 1957 by Nuky Fellows and Eleanor Wolf. Nuky had grown up on the island, a member of the pioneer Vinal family that arrived on the island in 1908. In 1981, Eleanor Wolf died and Nuky Fellows retired in 1984, so a parent volunteer board was formed to run the school. The building still houses a pre-school to Island youth after over 60 years!

Another long-time resident of the property is The Children's Dance Conservatory, directed by Susan Valencia, for over 25 years. This Royal Academy of Dance (RAD) school puts on a lovely youth Nutcracker performance every year which should not be missed. The Mercer Island Saddle Club reminds us of the wonderful rural past of Mercer Island. Horses are stabled and trained on the grounds and riders utilize the nearby trails of Pioneer Park for enjoyment.

1.5 mi   **Continue on 68ᵗʰ Street and soon you will see the Fire Station on your left and a great sculpture on your right.**

This piece called "Mythical Bird" was created by an award winning sculptor named Dudley Carter from Redmond Washington. Dudley Carter was born in Canada and worked in logging until the depression when he turned to art. His art is known internationally, and much of his work was in the form of totem poles (one of which can be found at the entrance to Marymoor Park). He used an axe to create his large works and continued to create new works until he died at the age of 100 in 1992. Do you see the raven, coyote, birds and female forms in this sculpture?

1.6 mi   **Next, you'll see the South End Shopping Center and the end of our walk.**

 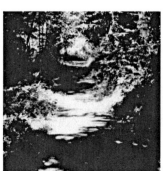 

"One who walks in another's tracks leaves no footprints."
Anonymous

Family Walk |
South End High Loop

Instead of heading to the grocery store during the hour you have waiting for practice to end at the South End Playfields, head out on this great walk complete with big views, hidden cut-thrus, and safe walking. You can manage it in your tennis shoes or with a stroller, so no excuses!

Rating: Family

Length: 2,8 miles

Terrain: Quiet residential streets, paved and graveled paths

Highlights: Hidden Cut-Thrus, big Mt. Rainier views, horses

Trailhead: Start at the South End Playfields on SE 78th St

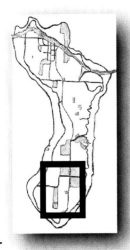

Guided Tour: South End High Loop

0.00 mi   Start at the South End playfields, using the restrooms if needed. Head across the street toward Lakeridge Elementary School, going right (west) on 78th Street and through the cut in the fence into the neighborhood called "The Lakes." Take a left on 81st Place SE.

The Lakes is a planned housing community that was built in the mid 1970s. The 40-acre development has built in "lakes that are designed to hold storm water, releasing it slowly downhill to the lake without impacting the city's minimal trail lines and ditches." This neighborhood is full of kids, and is "the place to be" (supervised of course) on Halloween.

0.2 mi   The road continues to the right, turning into 80th Place SE. This road has gorgeous fall color. Make sure to do this walk at least once just before the leaves start falling.

0.3 mi   Just past the grassy area, take a left on the gravel path, then a right at the split in the path, heading north.

This favorite path of neighborhood kids on foot or bikes runs the entire length of the Lakes.

0.5 mi   Continue straight on the path at the junction until the trail emerges onto a gravel drive that will take you to the end of 80th.

0.6 mi   When you reach the busy corner of 80th and 72nd, cross the street at the crosswalk taking care.

0.8 mi   At SE 71st take a right and head up two blocks, then taking a left on 82nd Ave SE.

1.2 mi   Cross SE 68th and then take a right on SE 67th Street and go up the little hill. At the end of SE 67th Street, you'll see a path to the right of the fire hydrant. Take the path, cutting through to Pioneer Park.

Turn-by-Turn Directions:

- **Start:** South End Playfields
- Right on SE 78th
- Cut-thru into Lakes, left on 81st Pl SE
- 87th Pl SE turns into 80th Pl SE
- Left on to gravel path, then right at junction
- Emerge at 80th Ave SE, Cross 72nd Street
- Right on SE 71st
- Left on 82nd Ave SE
- Right on SE 67th Street
- Cut-Thru to Pioneer Park
- Right on trail in Pioneer Park
- Left on trail along 68th Street
- Right at Sunnybeam on Island Crest Way
- Straight at Cut Thru
- Left on SE 82nd Street
- Right on 84th Ave SE
- Left on SE 78th
- **End:** South End Playfields

At 120 acres, Pioneer Park is the largest natural space on Mercer Island. Its three-40 acre natural woodland parcels give visitors a feel for what the Island must have looked like in the mid-1800's. Although the entire Island had been logged clean of its virgin timber by the turn of the century, the property is an amazing example of how our ecosystem naturally restores itself when left all alone. Many of the trees in the park are over 100 feet tall and 100 years old, while stumps from the original logging effort can still be found today.

The park property was privately owned until 1931 when it was willed to the University of Washington by Mrs. Maud Walker-Ames, whose family ironically was one of the most prominent and wealthy logging families in the Northwest. Interestingly, she also willed their family home to the UW, and the 40-room, 12,788 square foot, brick mansion—colloquially referred to as 808—is still home to the University President and his family, and acts as a bustling social venue for University events.

When Mercer Island was incorporated in 1960, the city started planning for a park system and learned that the "university properties" (as they were known) were available. The city passed a bond in 1964 to purchase the land to allow islanders to get out in nature. In 1969, it seemed imminent that 80 acres of the park would be cleared for a municipal golf course and the prospect came forth again in the 1980's with both efforts defeated.

The Park today contains 6.6 miles of trails for walking and limited trails for horseback riding, which have been kept in a natural state. An old, but still relevant detailed resource about the park is called "Pioneer Park—A Natural History" that can be found online (see Resources). It would be wonderful if the Mercer Island Parks and Recreation group did another revision to this guide as it really helps bring the Park alive.

1.3 mi   **Cross the street to enter Pioneer Park, take a right on the trail, then a left at the junction staying on the perimeter path that parallels 68ᵗʰ Street. The south end shopping center will be on your right.**
The Southend Shopping Center was opened in 1961, when the south end was still quite rural, amid a zoning and landscaping controversy. It was, in fact, the last rezoning and development plan done under county jurisdiction. After that the planning and design was managed by the islands' Town and City governments.

1.4 mi   **You'll see the Fire Station on your right (opened in 1961), and on your left is a great piece of art.**

This piece called "Mythical Bird" was created by an award winning sculptor named Dudley Carter from Redmond Washington. Dudley Carter was born in Canada and worked in logging until the depression when he turned to art. His art is know internationally, and much of his work was in the form of totem poles (one of which can be found at the entrance to Marymoor Park). He used an axe to create his large works and continued creating new works until he died at the age of 100 in 1992. Do you see the raven, coyote, birds and female forms in this sculpture?

Continue on the trail along SE 68ᵗʰ Street, to Lakeview School.

This historic building was built in 1918 when the local school district voted to build a schoolhouse by issuing local improvement bonds. All elementary grades were taught at the school and then students were ferried to Seattle or Bellevue for high school until 1941, when the roads had been improved enough to bus students to East Seattle School.mmThe small cottage on the property was built at the same time as the school to house the teacher. Today, it is the home of the Pioneer Park Youth Club's caretakers.

Today, the property is owned and managed by a small volunteer group, The Pioneer Youth Club, which started out as the "South End Improvement Club" a citizens group that was extremely active until the 1970's bringing services such as roads, water and power to south end residents. In 1974, the group traded the 10 acre parcel of land they owned (that now houses IMS, Lakeridge and the South Mercer Playfields) for this smaller tract that the school district owned—allowing new schools to be built on the South End of Mercer Island.

The 4.35 acre property is now home to Sunnybeam School, Mercer Island Saddle Club, and the Children's Dance Conservatory. Sunnybeam School was started in 1957 by Nuky Fellows and Eleanor Wolf. Nuky had grown up on the island, a member of the pioneer Vinal family that arrived on the island in

1908. In 1981, Eleanor Wolf died and Nuky Fellows retired in 1984, so a parent volunteer board formed to run the school. The building still houses a pre-school for Island youth after over 60 years!

Another long-time resident of the property is The Children's Dance Conservatory, directed by Susan Valencia, for over 25 years. This Royal Academy of Dance (RAD) school puts on a lovely youth Nutcracker performance every year which should not be missed. The Mercer Island Saddle Club reminds us of the wonderful rural past of Mercer Island. Horses are stabled and trained on the grounds and riders utilize the nearby trails of Pioneer Park for enjoyment.

Cut through the gravel parking lot to the horses and continue out the other gravel entrance to Island Crest Way and take a right, going south.

1.7 mi   **Soon you'll join up with the new Island Crest Trail that was completed in 2008.**

The trail makes this end of the Island much safer for walking. Along the way, you'll see two trails that veer off toward Wildwood Park—formerly known as "Tract A" and the location of the second off leash dog area on the Island (the other being at Luther Burbank Park.)

2.0 mi   **Past SE 78th, the road will dead end. Continue straight at the Island Heights Lane sign and down the little hill. The pavement will end and gravel begins and you will see a trail sign at the end.**

Take a moment to enjoy the view. It doesn't get any better than this! (I also enjoy the roses in this family's yard—a true green thumb lives there.) Out to the left is the location of one of the three sunken forests that are directly adjacent to Mercer Island. One is here near South Point, one near the west central shore, and one off the north shore. The trees still stand upright under the water. At the turn of the century, they became a hazard to water craft, so they were cut off 15 to 20 feet below the surface of the water by a wire drag towed by a ship. Some believe the forests slid into the water in a massive land slide and others believe that they stand where they grew, but were covered by the waters of the lake as it rose.

2.2 mi   **The trail will take you to the junction SE 82nd and SE 80th. Stay to the left on SE 82nd Street. Along this road, you'll see a funny little trail on your right which cuts-thru to SE 80th. Continue straight and then take a right on 84th Ave SE. Cross over on the raised sidewalk (thanks to the Lakeridge parents that have done so much work to make this area safer for walking.)**

2.8 mi   **At SE 78th, take a left and you'll be back where you started at the Mercer Island Play Fields.**

"I don't really think, I just walk."
Paris Hilton

Moderate Walk |
South End Big Loop

This long hike is spectacular on clear days as it offers amazing views of Mt. Rainier and Lake Washington. Along the way you'll see why locals love Mercer Island—as you'll travel lovely neighborhoods, expansive parks, and charming wooded trails. A large portion of the hike is along the south tip of the island on East and West Mercer Way, which generally is pretty quiet, but for the best possible experience do try and avoid commute times. This hike ends with a nice elevation gain, so pace yourself!

Rating: Ambitious

Length: 4.0 miles

Terrain: Residential streets, parks, and wooded trails.

Highlights: Spectacular views of Lake Washington and Mt. Rainier, hidden cut-thrus, beautiful neighborhoods.

Trailhead: Start at the South Mercer Playfields

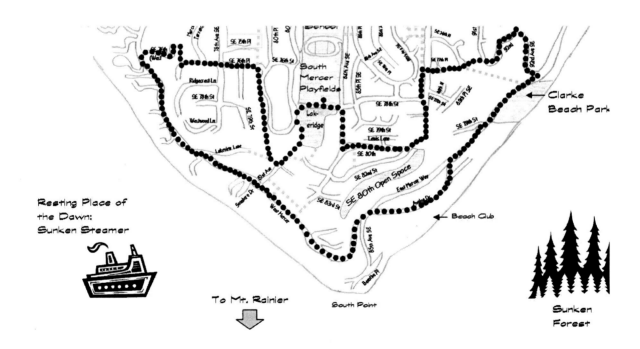

Guided Tour: South End Big Loop

0.0 mi   This hike starts at the South Mercer Playfields. From the parking lot head south toward Lakeridge Elementary, taking a right on SE 78th Street and going past the back parking lot of the school.

This ten acre parcel that now houses IMS, Lakeridge and the South Mercer Playfields, was once owned by the "South End Improvement Club" a citizens group started to bring services such as roads, water and power to south end residents. In 1974, the group traded the site for the School Districts Lakeview School and smaller 4.35 acres parcel. The group was extremely active until the 1970's, and in 1975 it changed its name to the Pioneer Youth Club. This small volunteer organization still owns and manages the Lakeview School property that houses Sunnybeam School, Mercer Island Saddle Club and the Children's Dance Conservatory.

0.1 mi   Just before the cut through to the Lakes, take a left on the gravel path and go to the far south west corner of the Lakeridge School grounds, skirting around the portables to get there. The trail will begin to the right of the undercover playground area.

0.2 mi   The trail will emerge into a neighborhood. Continue down the path between house #8280 and #8285, to the right of the bench. You will start dropping quickly as this path is very steep.

0.3 mi   You'll come out at the top of 81st Ave SE. Continue down the road until you come to a junction. Then take a right up the hill.

Turn-by-Turn Directions:

- **Start:** South Mercer Playfields
- Southwest to Lakeridge Elementary
- Take trail that goes on the right side of the school, behind the portables
- Emerge at the end of SE 82nd
- Continue down the steep path to your right
- Emerge at the top of 81st Ave SE
- At the first junction, take a right up the hill
- At the two path signs, take the one to the right that goes up the hill
- Continue on the long path that skirts the west side of the Lakes
- Continue straight when you join 80th Ave
- Then take a left back onto the path
- At SE 76th take a left.
- Cross Mercer Terrance and continue until SE 76th ends.
- At the mailboxes, take the path to your right, winding down the hill and to your left.
- Emerge at the top of SE 76th. Continue down the hill to West Mercer Way
- Go left on West Mercer Way
- Continue straight as West Mercer Way turns into East Mercer Way
- At Avalon Drive take a right, dipping down and back up to East Mercer Way
- Go right on East Mercer Way.
- Pass Clarke Beach and then take a left on SE 76th Street
- Go up the hill until the road ends. Take a left across the little stream, emerging on 91st Ave SE
- At the crest of the hill, just past #7427 take a left
- Take the trail on your right between the wooden fences
- At the cul-de-sac continue across and take the stairs between two hedges. Emerge at SE 77th Pl
- Go straight to Island Crest Way and take a left
- Continue past SE 78th until Island Crest dead ends
- Take the path, emerging at SE 82nd and SE 80th.
- Go straight on SE 80th
- Take a right at 84th Ave SE
- Go left on SE 78th Street
- **End:** South Mercer Playfields

0.4 mi You'll come to two path signs on either side of house #8136. The one to the left takes you past a nice view of Lake Washington and ends at a trail down a driveway (#7950) that has a strategically placed flower pot in front of the trail post at the top of Lakeview Lane. We'll leave that one to another day and take the one to the right which winds up the hill to a trail that runs the western border of the Lakes.

You'll pass some spectacular Rhododendrons that bloom pink in the spring as you follow the trail north. You'll have the Lakes on your right, and some large flat yards on your left. The Lakes is a planned housing community that was built in the mid 1970s. The 40-acre development has built in "lakes that are designed to hold storm water, releasing it slowly downhill to the lake without impacting the city's minimal trail lines and ditches." This neighborhood is full of kids, and is "the place to be" (supervised of course) on Halloween.

0.5 mi Eventually, the trail will join the sidewalk at the Lakes and then will veer of left again at a trail sign. You could continue south on the trail which eventually ends at 80th Ave SE, but instead we'll take a left off the trail onto SE 76th St.

0.8 mi Heading down SE 76th St, you'll cross 79th Ave SE, 78th Ave SE, and Mercer Terrance Drive. The road will end at a bank of mailboxes and a trail will appear to your right.

0.9 mi Go under the trellis and onto the trail which hooks a left and emerges in the West Firs neighborhood at the top of SE 76th Street.

1.0 mi At one mile into the hike you'll emerge at the West Firs sign on West Mercer Way. Take a left going south on West Mercer Way.

1.1 mi There's an old grove of Madronna trees along this stretch, and some big western views. When you get a good view of the lake, you'll be looking at the final resting spot for one little piece of history.

The ferry Dawn serviced Mercer Island until the floating bridge was built, making ferry service obsolete. From the late 1800's until the opening of the Floating Bridge in 1940, ferry service was the lifeblood of Mercer Island residents, moving commuters, students, visitors and provisions back and forth from Seattle to Mercer Island. The ferry boat Dawn ferried passengers from Leschi Park to Mercer Island from 1914 until 1938, stopping at docks along the west side of the island. Captain John L. Anderson built the Dawn to replace the aging Cyrene that had serviced the Island for 20 years.

The Dawn was 55 feet long, carried up to 250 passengers, and was able to operate with a crew of one or two. On Christmas Eve of 1924 in an 80 mile-an-hour gale, the Dawn broke her mooring lines and sunk. She was raised, repaired and put back into service for another 14 years before being retired in 1938 where she was docked at Rainier Beach. In 1946, the Dawn was deemed a hazard to the community and taken out into the middle of the lake and sunk.

The wreckage of the Dawn can still be found by divers in a relatively shallow 115 feet of water here in front of you, between the south end of Mercer Island and Rainier Beach. It is described by those that have seen it as sitting upright and in generally good shape. It is considered a spooky wreck to dive because it is clearly identifiable and can be entered.

1.4 mi Lakeview Lane has that hidden trail up to Lakeridge (go up the driveway of house #7950—you'll see the path sign behind that strategically placed planter). It's a good one to remember for another day. The next street, marked with addresses 8130-8182 and Lakeridge Heights, is the bottom of the steep decline we took earlier on the hike. Today though, we'll continue on West Mercer.

1.7 mi   **Continuing on West Mercer, you'll see a little path, and then a marked path—Fluery Trail.** Fluery Trail is one of my favorite trails on the Island. The first time I happened upon it, I was so surprised. There are a couple of ponds up in the woods to the left of Fluery Trail as well, making it a fun adventure for another day. The trail is named for Alfred Fluery who was described as "Mr. Everything" from when he arrived on the island in 1933 until he and his wife left the island in 1977 for a Seattle retirement home. For 44 years he accomplished a great deal by being active in libraries, roads, schools, playfields, firefighting, and utilities—a model of civic betterment. He died in 1993 at 103, active very nearly to the end. The Fluery's lived at the top of the trail.

2.1 mi   **Soon West Mercer Way changes to East Mercer Way, and you start heading north where you'll come to the sign for SE 87ᵗʰ and Benotho Place.**

The street name change is at South Point—the location of one of the most chilling tales of Mercer Island. This area was known by early Island residents as "Murder Point" or Deadman's Bay" because of a longtime Mercer Island mystery which dates back to 1886 when heavy logging activity was underway on Mercer Island.

James Coman, a County Commissioner who was firmly against illegal claims of public land and a 12 year old family friend died over a claim-jumping accusation with Mercer Island resident George Miller. After a threat was issued, the two were never to be seen alive again. Later, their boat was found off South Point with bloodstains and later their bullet-ridden bodies were found in the lake in the same area. In a sensational series of trials, Miller was acquitted. Legend has it that George Miller confessed to the murders on his deathbed and that the murder weapon was later found on his property.

The east side of South Point was the location of the county dock which was the landing for launches and later for ferries to Rainier Beach, Renton and Kenneydale. Ben Lindren and Otho Cochran bought a tract of Northern Pacific Railroad land in the 1920's. When they platted lots they gave their names Ben-Otho to the project and it is still known as Benotho Beach. South Point is still a public access point today. You'll see the sign for Benotho Place along the way.

2.2 mi   **Take a right on Avalon Drive, dipping down parallel to East Mercer Way, and soon on your right you'll see the sign for the private Mercer Island Beach Club.**

This 8 acre property was bought in the 1930's by the Lion's Club from the Northern Pacific Railway. They created a camp for under-privileged city kids which operated for several years. The coming of the bridge and then the war closed the camp, but during and after the war, the property was used by convalescing soldiers from Fort Lewis. In 1953 200 families from the South End Club, which was formed in the 20's to advocate for South End residents, bought the property and formed the Beach Club. In 1966 the clubhouse, swimming pool and tennis courts were built, and in 2006 the beach club was again improved to a year-round facility. The caretaker's cottage from the original Lion's Club camp still remains on the property, relatively intact.

2.5 mi   **The road will scoop back up again and join East Mercer Way. Take a right on East Mercer, crossing to face traffic.** Soon, if it's clear, you'll see a spectacular view of Mt. Rainier. Known simply as "the mountain" it never ceases to amaze. I love how locals refer to it so regularly. "Did you see the mountain today?" "Oh look,, the mountain is out." The National Park is over 200,000 acres about 50 miles southeast of here. It's about 97% wilderness and is the tallest peak in the south 48 at 14,410 feet. It's an active volcano that last erupted about 150 years ago.

2.8 mi   **On your right you'll see Clarke Beach and on the left will be a 7700 block sign at the street directly across from Clarke Beach.** Clarke Beach honors Island pioneer Mabel Clarke who came to the island in 1907, and who still has family members that remain Island residents today. This property was not the Clarke's land however, they settled on the west side of the island, just south of the historic East Seattle neighborhood.

In the early 1900's, the Clarke Beach Park property had a large mansion with landscaped grounds and was known as the Rhoades Estate. In the early years, three sisters and a brother lived there, but during the 40's and 50's it was owned by the Charles Morris family and the house was the scene of many South End gatherings. The building was torn down when the City bought the property for a park, but some of the beautiful estate shrubs and trees, like the monkey puzzle tree, remain.

Within the last 10 years there was a trail that cut up this the road on your left marked 7700 block through the hillside to the Tarrywood neighborhood and on to Island Crest. It was a wonderful way to get safely from the South End of Mercer Island to the beach. Sadly, the stairs became unsafe after a mudslide, although the public easement remains. I'd love to see the City put a little work and cash into getting this route back.

Continue past Clarke Beach and take a left on SE 76th Street (you will see a sign that says to 92nd Ave SE and a trail marker.) This road connects to a trail system that takes you all the way up through the Tarywood neighborhood to Island Crest Way. In 1933, the Girl Scout Council established Camp Tarywood here in the forest above East Mercer. The camp had a main lodge, tent platforms, and open air cabins. The campers came to true wilderness. The camp was sold in 1969 to the school district and the shore area was purchased by the city to become part of Clarke Beach. The name remains on the upland tract, now Tarywood Estates.

2.9 mi   **Continue heading up the road along the little creek. Soon you'll see a log barrier. After the barrier go left over the creek (you'll see a Tarrywood Trail sign). Head up the street which turns into 91st Ave SE.**

3.3 mi   **At the crest of the hill, just past #7427, take a left. You'll see the trail on your right between two wooden fences. Go up the stairs. You'll emerge at SE 77th Place. Continue straight to Island Crest Way and take a left.**

3.5 mi   **Past SE 78th, the road will dead end. Continue straight at the Island Heights Lane sign and down the little hill. The pavement will end and gravel begins and you will see a trail sign at the end.** Take a moment to enjoy the view. It doesn't get any better than this! I also enjoy the roses in this family's yard—a true green thumb lives there. Out to the left is the location of one of the three sunken forests that are directly adjacent to Mercer Island. One is here near South Point, one near the west central shore, and one off the north shore. The trees still stand upright under the water. At the turn of the century, they became a hazard to water craft, so they were cut off 15 to 20 feet below the surface of the water by a wire drag towed by a ship. Some believe the forests slid into the water in a massive land slide and others believe that they stand where they grew, but were covered with the waters of the lake as it rose.

3.7 mi   **The trail will take you to the junction SE 82nd and SE 80th. Stay to the right on SE 80th Street.** Along this road, you'll see a funny little trail on your left which cuts-thru to SE 82nd. **Continue straight and then take a right on 84th Ave SE. Cross over on the raised sidewalk** (thanks to the Lakeridge parents who have done so much work to make this area safer for walking.

4.0 mi   **At SE 78th, take a left and you'll be back where you started at the Mercer Island Play Fields.**

"I walk where I choose to walk."
Norman Thomas

"Walking isn't a lost art: one must, by some means, get to the garage."
Evan Esar

Section Three

From Here to There

On an island that is only 6.2 square miles—five miles long and less than two miles across at its widest—everything is very close when you're on foot. You just have to know how to get there! This section will give you some great routes to get from here to there. Each route gives you Turn-By-Turn Directions and a map to make it easy.

Routes:

From Here to There |
Slater Park to Roanoke Inn

VIA: SE 22nd Street Cut-Thru
MILES: 1.5 miles
NOTES: 22nd provides a hidden path between East
            Seattle and North Mercer with gorgeous
            views along the way.

DIRECTIONS:
* **Depart**: Slater Park
* North On 60th Ave SE
* Under I-90 Bridge
* Right on SE 22nd St
* Continue on path at end of SE 22nd St
* Up the hill at end of the path
* Left on West Mercer Way
* Right on 72nd Ave SE
* **Arrive**: Roanoke Inn on right.

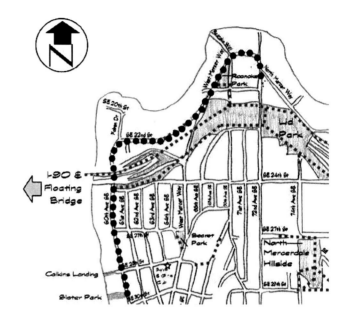

From Here to There |
Roanoke Inn to Luther Burbank Park

VIA: Outdoor sculpture gallery.
MILES: 1.1 miles
NOTES: This urban route has a lot going on along the way.

DIRECTIONS:
* **Depart**: Roanoke Inn
* Go south on 72nd Ave SE
* Just before overpass, take a left into Lid Park.
* Go right past the baseball fields and then left at the path towards the playground
* Cross the street at 76th Ave SE and continue on the path
* Cross the street at 77th Ave SE and enter the sculpture garden
* At 80th Ave cross the street and continue on the sidewalk to Island Crest Way
* Cross Island Crest Way and take the path on your left
* Take a left into park, winding over the freeway.
* Take ramp down the hill toward Luther Burbank Park
* Take a right on I-90 Trail
* Take a left at the opening and cross North Mercer Way
* Take a left on North Mercer Way
* **Arrive**: Luther Burbank Park on right.

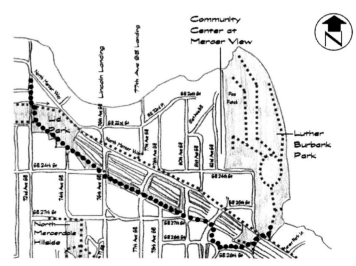

From Here to There |
Bicentennial Park to Proctor Landing

VIA: SE 32nd St Cut-Thru
MILES: .75 miles
NOTES: 32nd provides a direct route from town to East Seattle. It's the best, most direct route, taken by the early Mercer Island Settlers.

DIRECTIONS:

- **Depart:** Bicentennial Park
- Up hill on stairs
- Straight at every path.
- Emerge at 32nd St
- Across First Hill on 32nd St
- After Park, continue down 32nd
- Continue on path
- Cross East Mercer Way
- Continue on 32nd St
- Arrive: Proctor Landing

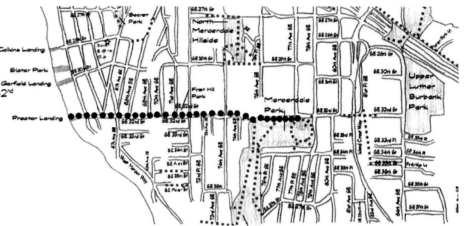

From Here to There |
Lid Park Courts to Boys & Girls Club

VIA: 68th Ave SE Cut-Thru
MILES: 0.8 miles
NOTES: The 69th Cut-Thru is a direct way through neighborhoods instead of on busy West Mercer Way.

DIRECTIONS:

- Depart: Lid Park tennis courts
- Go south on 70th Ave SE
- Cross busy SE 24th St
- Veer right at 68th Ave SE
- Continue on the trail through 68th Ave SE
- Right down the path down SE 28th Street
- Cross Busy West Mercer Way
- Left on West Mercer Way
- Left on SE 28th St
- Arrive: Boys & Girls Club

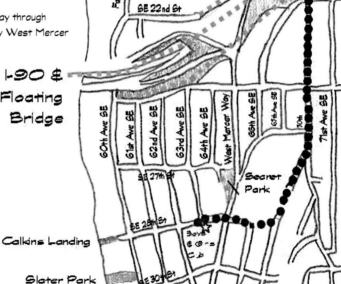

From Here to There |
Library to Mercerwood Shore Club

VIA: Shorewood Drive
MILES: 1.1 miles
NOTES: Nice, direct route with little or no traffic.

DIRECTIONS:
- **Start:** Youth Theater Northwest
- Head north on 88th Ave SE
- When you get to Shorewood Drive, go right
- Pass E Lexington Way
- Right on SE Shorewood Drive
- Left on i-90 Trail
- Cross North Mercer at Crosswalk
- Right into Luther Burbank Park
- **End:** Luther Burbank Park

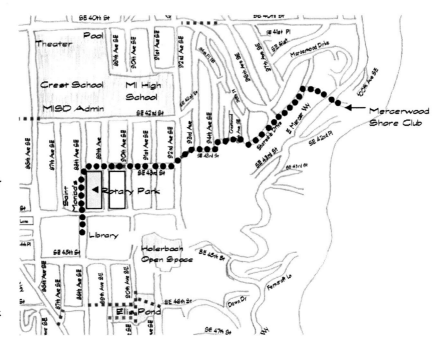

From Here to There |
Youth Theater to Luther Burbank Park

VIA: Snake Hill
MILES: 1 mile
NOTES: It's all downhill and skips the Island Crest Way traffic.

DIRECTIONS:
- **Start:** MI High School
- Go West on SE 42nd Street
- Cross 86th Ave SE and continue on trail
- Got right on 85th Ave SE
- Carefully cross SE 40th Street and go left
- Turn right into Clise Park on the trail
- Turn right on Island Crest Way
- Continue straight at 84th Ave SE
- Continue around the curve (left) after passing Upper Luther Burbank Park
- Continue into town at SE 28th Street
- **End:** North End of Town

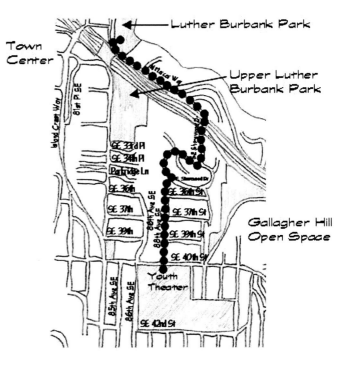

From Here to There |
High School to North End of Town

VIA: Snake Hill
MILES: 1 mile
NOTES: It's all downhill and skips the Island Crest Way traffic.

DIRECTIONS:
- Start: MI High School
- Go West on SE 42nd Street
- Cross 86th Ave SE and continue on trail
- Got right on 85th Ave SE
- Carefully cross SE 40th Street and go left
- Turn right into Clise Park on the trail
- Turn right on Island Crest Way
- Continue straight at 84th Ave SE
- Continue around the curve (left) after passing Upper Luther Burbank Park
- Continue into town at SE 28th Street
- End: North End of Town

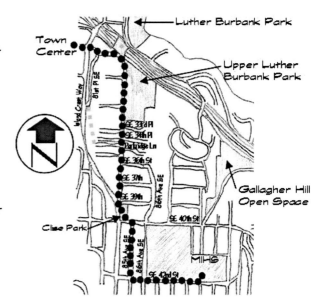

From Here to There |
Library to Island Park School

VIA: Ellis Pond
MILES: 1.0 miles
NOTES: A really pleasant walk—through Ellis pond with its ducks!

DIRECTIONS:
- Start: Library
- Left on 88th Ave SE
- Left on SE 45th Street
- Right on 90th Ave SE
- Through Ellis Pond—on trail just to the right of the pond
- Emerge on 90th Ave SE
- Cross SE 47th, 48th and 50th Streets
- Left on Island Crest Way
- Right at crosswalk
- End: Island Park Elementary

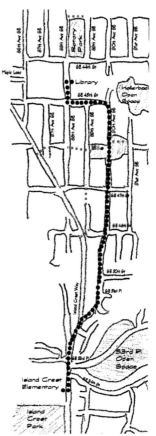

From Here to There |
Island Crest Park to Groveland Park

VIA: SE 59th Street Cut-Thru
MILES: 0,5miles
NOTES: You won't believe how close this is—it
          might even be faster to walk than drive!

DIRECTIONS:

- Start: Island Crest Park
- Go down trail off of main parking lot
- Cross the suspension bridge
- Left at the end of it.
- Right, then right again at the junctions.
- Emerge at 84th Ave SE and cross the street
- Down SE 59th Street
- ½ block down, look for the path on your right (sign is hard to see) and go down the path
- Emerge at driveway that leads to West Mercer Way
- Left on West Mercer Way
- Cross street and take a right on SE 57th
- End: Groveland Beach Park

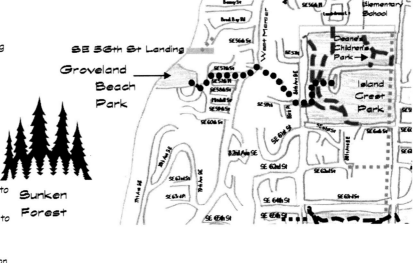

From Here to There |
Sunnybeam to Clarke Beach

VIA: 77th Place Cut-Thru
MILES: 1.1 miles
NOTES: Fun, hidden trail through the Tarrywood neighborhood.

DIRECTIONS:

- Start: Sunnybeam School
- Head south on the trail along Island Crest
- At the end of Pioneer Park, cross back on the west side of Island Crest and continue on the gravel trail.
- Left at SE 77th Place
- Follow the path sign, emerging through the fence at the end of SE 74th Pl
- Go across the cul-de-sac and continue on the trail to 91st Ave SE
- At the end of the trail, veer left to hit 92nd Pl SE
- Go right on 92nd Pl SE to the end
- Cross the creek on the trail and go right on 92nd,
- Emerging at East Mercer Way and go right
- End: Clarke Beach

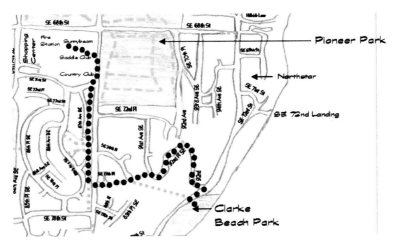

From Here to There |
Clarke Beach to South End Shopping

VIA: 92nd Ave Cut-Thru
MILES: 0.9 miles
NOTES: One you probably
              won't happen upon on
              your own

DIRECTIONS:
- Start: Clarke Beach
- Go right on East Mercer Way
- Left at 92nd up hill
- At the end of 92nd, continue straight on the path
- At the top of the path, go right on 92nd Ave SE and continue to Pioneer Park
- Go right on the Pioneer Park trail, curving left along SE 68th St, staying on the park edge
- Cross Island Crest Way
- End: South End Shopping Center

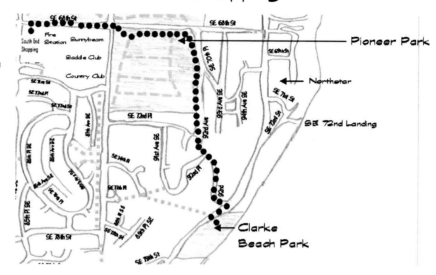

From Here to There |
South Mercer Playfield to Beach Club

VIA: Fluery Trail
MILES: 0.8 miles
NOTES: I love Fluery Trail—and
              unexpected retreat!

DIRECTIONS:
- Start: South Mercer Playfield
- Left on SE 78th St, then right (south) on 84th Ave SE
- Down hill to the end of the street
- Continue on Fluery trail, down stairs
- Emerge at West Mercer Way, take a left
- Continue straight when West Mercer Way turns into East Mercer Way
- Right on Avalon Drive
- Right into Beach Club
- End: Beach Club

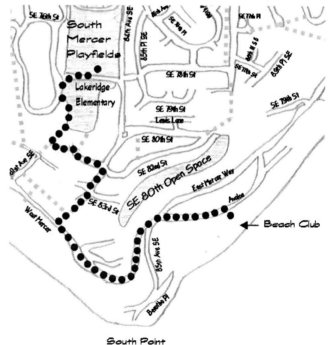

"Now, it used to be I ran to get where I was going. I never thought it would take me anywhere."

Forrest Gump

Beyond this Guide

Contact Us

For more information about this guide and walking on Mercer Island, check out our blog at: www.walkmercerisland.com, or contact us via email at info@walkmercerisland.com.

Additional Copies

Additional copies of this guide can be purchased for $20/copy at local stores, online at www.walkmercerisland.com, or by sending a check for $25.00 ($20/copy + plus tax + postage) to: Walk! Mercer Island, PO Box 1658, Mercer Island, WA 98040. Volume discounts are available for promotional or educational activities. For additional information contact us at: info@walkmercerisland.com.

Errors, Adjustments and Recommendations

Although I've done my best to check and re-check the information in this guide, I'm certain to have gotten a few things wrong. You're help in making it even better are appreciated. Submit your changes via email to info@walkmercerisland.com.

Proceeds

Walk! | Mercer Island is a division of Launch, LLC a fully owned and operated by Kris Kelsay. A portion of the proceeds from this guide are donated to the Mercer Island Open Space Conservatory or Mercer Island Historical Society.

Bibliography

City of Mercer Island, Government Web Site, Open Space and Parks & Trails pages. www.mercergov.org, 2009.
City of Mercer Island, Mercer Island Leash Laws, http://www.mercergov.org/Page.asp?NavID=1999.
City of Mercer Island Arts Council, Public Art, pamphlet.
City of Mercer Island Parks and Recreation, City of Mercer Island Washington Trails Guide, pamphlet 1993.
City of Mercer Island Parks and Recreation, Mercer Island Parks System Guide, http://www.mercergov.org/Files/MI PARKSGUIDE.PDF, 2008.
City of Mercer Island Parks and Recreation, Pioneer Park: A Natural History, http://www.mercergov.org/files/ppfmpF-Qcomp.pdf, 1990.
Gellatly, Judy. Mercer Island, Mercer Island Bicentennial Committee, 1977.
Images of Seattle.org, Public Artwork on Mercer Island. http://www.imagesofseattle.org/Artwork of Mercer Island/Artwork of Mercer Island.html#, 2009.
McDonald, Lucile. The Lake Washington Story, Superior Publishing Company, Seattle, Washington, 1979.
Mercer Island Chamber of Commerce, 7605 SE 27th St #109, Mercer Island, WA 98040.
Mercer Island, Chamber of Commerce, Discovery Map of Mercer Island 2008.
Mercer Island Historical Society. Web Site www.mihistory.org, and Newsletters. PO Box 111, Mercer Island, WA. 206-236-3274.
The Seattle Times, A Hidden Past: An Exploration of Eastside History, 2000.
My Parks and Recreation, www.myparksandrecreation.com

"Perhaps the truth depends on a walk around the lake."
Wallace Stevens

Acknowledgements

So many people were so very helpful in the making of this book. Phone calls and emails led to new contacts and resources. I discovered quickly how small our community really is.   The ladies at the Mercer Island Chamber of Commerce were especially helpful and put me in touch with numerous resources, and the city employees were always helpful (although busy!)

Thanks to Neil Fanger, Steve Litzow, and Dino Annest, for meeting with me, offering their ideas and acting as sounding board through the process. Also Wayne Gullstad who actually tramped around the woods of Pioneer Park with me teaching me how to identify the different trees and looking for logging artifacts, and Paul West (one of the city arborists) who pointed me to a great Pioneer Park resource. Robin Newell, fellow art docent at Island Park Elementary shared her research on the art pieces, Lucy Phillips who told me some of her secrets about the north end, and Diana Low who gave me encouragement and ideas for the next guide.

I thank the fellow walkers that I met along the trail—wondering what I was doing with a measuring wheel! They were always so encouraging—talking about their favorite places—the wildlife they had recently seen, and the lost trails that they missed. On the journey I ran into two ladies on the dock at Luther Burbank Park who told me all about the beavers and turtles they had seen over the years; couples walking who had lived on the island, 30, 40, and even 50 years; a famous modern architect that pointed me toward some reading—all were out there walking our Mercer Island trails.

I especially want to thank my daughter Shea who handled the measuring wheel on many of the hikes, my mother, Dee Kurtz, for reading and editing the book, my son Connor for appreciating the history I was discovering, and my husband Todd for tolerating this amount of time and work for a book with a very small target market!

About the Author

As a long-time resident of Mercer Island and an avid walker and hiker, Kris Kelsay has been exploring the extensive public paths and park system on foot for close to 20 years.

A high technology marketing consultant by trade, Kris has written copy for a countless number of business plans, web sites and brochures. However, *Walk! Mercer Island* is her first attempt at a literary endeavor. While she's helped start 3D mapping and location-based technology companies—she had really never attempted to map anything herself by hand. She loves the outdoors—rain or shine—and spends as much time as possible there.

She lives in a house on a hill in the woods hidden away on the east side of Mercer Island with her adventurous husband and two great kids.

Made in the USA